Here's to: "happy cooking" by my
favorite gourmet chef
.... and .... even better—
"happier eating" by her husband!

With best wishes at Christmas,
,1970
.... Mary Lou

Yvonne Young Tarr

Illustrations by TIM GAYDOS

THE *Ten* *Minute*

GOURMET

Cookbook

Lyle Stuart ◄ *New York*
1965

Library of Congress Catalog Card Number 65–12352
Published by Lyle Stuart, Inc.
239 Park Avenue South, New York 3
Manufactured in the United States of America
by H. Wolff, New York
Designed by Marshall Lee

SECOND PRINTING, MAY 1967

. . . To my sons Jon and Nick who learned about gourmet cooking the hard way.

Contents

Foreword

A new way to gourmet!

 Stop!

Just this once read the foreword to your cookbook. It is important to you if you intend to get the most out of it: for herein lies a new way to Gourmet.

For far too many years gourmet cooking has been spoken of in reverent whispers. For far too long many gourmet cooks have frightened away the competition by discussing food with more "inside phrases" than are used on Madison Avenue at high noon. It's *Sauce Bechamel* this and *Montmorency* that when all that needed to be said was "cream sauce" and "with cherries."

Good recipes were usually guarded with enough secrecy and mistrust to put the Society of Black Magic to shame. And why?

Simply to hide the fact that cooking, even gourmet cooking, is easy. And it is!

Look at it this way. Nearly every day of their lives, busy Italian and French and German and Spanish mothers cook what we call gourmet dishes. Look through any gourmet cookbook. The dishes that are mentioned are most often what father gets for supper in some foreign land. To you and me they are exotic and glamorous but, to the woman who is cooking them in some far-off place, they are just tonight's steak and French fries. And conversely, of course, the ordinary dinners you cook are rare and exotic to them, so you see, you are already a gourmet cook to someone, perhaps that housewife in Brazil who is only having Angu Mineiro* for dinner tonight. So don't, for heaven's sake, let the thought of gourmet cooking intimidate you.

When I first started to cook, I opened a cookbook and made a crab soufflé. It turned out perfectly. No one had ever told me I should be afraid to try a soufflé. At that time I hadn't any idea it was the dish of kings. It just sounded good. After I had soufflés in several good restaurants and had heard the "Oooooos" and "Ahhhhhs" that accompanied them, I became so terrified that I didn't try one again for many years. And yet, from the first time I made one to the present day, I have never had a failure with a soufflé, simply because cooking is easy. If you can read you can cook—and this book proves it!

Here, for the first time so far as I know, is a collection of delicious gourmet recipes, none of which is really complex. They are nothing but beautiful, mouth-watering, unusual dishes which, although they take ten minutes or less to cook, are actually indistinguishable from their hard-to-prepare counterparts.

* Brazilian Lamb stew.

You'll find that none of them is hard to understand. This book doesn't tackle soufflés or French pastries. It isn't necessary. There are enough marvelous gourmet dishes that are ridiculously easy to make, especially with the techniques available today. Granted that when most gourmet dishes were invented, hours of preparation were necessary. But that was before canning, frozen foods, and modern appliances. How foolish we would be if we refused to use a blender just because Henry VIII's favorite chef didn't have one.

We who use this book have no such prejudices. We are concerned only with preparing gourmet dishes in a minimum amount of time and with maximum results. Any short cut we can take, providing it does not alter the quality of the dish we are cooking, is fine with us.

More important than the mere aspect of time, however, is the fact that these recipes really work, and not just occasionally, but each and every time. And what's more, they work with a minimum of confusion if you use this book properly. And by properly, I mean if you will get in the habit of following the carefully worked out, step-by-step directions.

You'll note, for example, that each recipe begins with a complete list of the ingredients and implements necessary to prepare it. (Naturally, cooking time begins once these items have been assembled.) These ingredient and implement lists are here to make your job as easy as possible and to speed up the time it takes to do the actual cooking as well. Get into the habit of using these lists properly and you'll discover what a boon they can be. No more searching for that missing spice while the onions get too brown, no more turning the kitchen upside down looking for the can opener only to find it fifteen minutes and one burned omelet later, propping open the kitchen window.

Get into the "assemble first" habit and your cooking will go faster and smoother, your food will be properly cooked, and you'll be a lot more relaxed and happy about it too.

Incidentally, another helpful feature to be found here is the "two-plus" system employed for feeding more than two guests. For example, while every recipe in this book is geared for two, merely add half a recipe more for each additional guest you expect, and cook away.

But one word of warning. As I've mentioned before, the object of cooking even in a short time is to obtain the most satisfactory results. Don't try to set any speed records in the beginning. Deliberately slow down when cooking a dish the first time. Later when you are more familiar with the recipes you will find yourself speeding along and many dishes will take even less than ten minutes to prepare. Until then be content with merely cooking superb creations—every time.

But even above and beyond cooking, this book is intended to point the way to a more rewarding way of fulfilling your role as a gracious hostess. What good if your food is great but your kitchen sees more of you than your guests? On the other hand, who will care to come again if you are a darling hostess but dinner is dreadful? Who indeed? The answer lies in a perfect combination of the two. Now you can create the dinner of your dreams from the correct wine to the most delicate garnish, every time, and still have time for your guests to enjoy you, your personality, your charm, your hospitality. After all, that's what they came for, that's what they are entitled to, and that's what you will be able to give them with the help of this book.

A teacupful of tips

If you have something more important to do right now, such as whipping up a tantalizing tidbit, by all means do it. If you haven't and you'd like a few thoughts, tips, and assorted good-sense suggestions gleaned from 14 years of gourmet cooking, do by all means read this.

I don't intend to rant on and fill your brain with hundreds of bits of information, most of which you will forget in a moment or less. When it comes to cooking, the phrases "learn from experience," "trial and error," and "learn the hard way" are trite but true. It would take thousands of words to describe accurately how it looks when a sauce "coats a spoon" or how thick a sauce is when it has "thickened slightly." These, I'll admit, are vague terms at best, but when you are cooking and suddenly, right on cue, a spoon becomes "coated" just as it says in the recipe, you automatically join the inner circle of cooks who "know" about coated spoons.

You need a good cookbook

Without doubt the most important single aid in good cooking is a good cookbook: one that you can rely upon. I have quite a few cookbooks, some of which are better than others. Some I know will produce recipes that work. Every time! Others, I have learned from experience, have recipes that will need "doctoring" as I go along. A sauce may have to be thickened a little more or a flame may have to be lowered to prevent a cheese dish from turning "mealy."

This is generally no disaster for an old hand at cooking but for a beginner it can cause anything from heartbreak to complete and utter panic, depending upon who is waiting hungrily at table.

The first cookbook I bought after I was married was a costly but famous compilation of a thousand recipes. "A thousand recipes? A bargain!" I thought. "How clever of me!" True it was expensive—but in the long run, with all those recipes . . .

I hadn't been clever at all! Nothing could have been more disappointing than that cookbook. There were so many tantalizing recipes to try, and try them I did with great patience and precision, but somehow they all cooked up into near misses. Either my "taster" was not tasting properly or gourmet food was just not as exciting as I had heard. What was wrong? Could it be—as I was afraid it might be—I?

At this moment, for all the world as it happens in fairy tales or television commercials, enter my mother with a skimpy little, unimpressive looking cookbook. Out of mere good manners I tried it and found to my delight that anything I fixed from that book was sheer ambrosia.

The secret is in the testing

I have tried many cookbooks from that time to this. Some always "worked," some "worked" some of the time, and others never "worked" without my stepping in to correct something along the way, but until I wrote a cookbook myself I never realized why some perform perfectly and others do not. Now that I know the secret it seems so obvious I blush to think it never occurred to me before. The secret is in the testing. My reliable little cookbook that worked so hard and well for me had been written by one man who took pride in every recipe and tested each with loving care. It is that conscientious concentration on testing that makes the difference in the performance of a cookbook.

Beware the large, stilted cookbooks!

If you are a brand new cook beware the large, stilted cookbooks that are little more than detailed listings of all the gourmet dishes in the world. Just because a dish is 400 years old does not mean there is only one way to cook it. Common sense alone will tell that the more hundreds and hundreds of recipes a cookbook has the less time is taken testing each one. These large compilations are fine for the expert but for the beginner or the "sometime" gourmet cook it is best to buy smaller cookbooks that have had more individual attention. For example, every recipe in this, *The Ten-Minute Gourmet Cookbook,* has been tested anywhere from 4 to 20 times with pencil firmly behind ear, pot firmly in hand, and burns on the fingers to prove it. Cookbooks that are made up of separate recipes contributed by individual cooks or books that consist of recipes served as specialities of famous restaurants are usually excellent also. These again contain special recipes that have actually been proved to be not only delectable but predictable too. Reputations ride on every recipe.

. . . *courage! Don't be afraid of anything!*

The second most important element in cooking is courage. Fortify yourself with a cookbook that has taken the trouble to be precise, and forge ahead courageously. Don't be afraid of anything! Pick out a recipe, purchase the necessary ingredients, assemble the proper utensils, allow yourself plenty of time, concentrate, and cook away! Nothing can happen but delicious food. The world doesn't depend upon the outcome of your meal. No heads will roll if your entrée isn't precisely the way you want it. As a matter of fact in most cases your guests probably do not dine nearly as well at home, so for your own sake relax!

Be a guest at your own party

If I were Queen Of All The Kitchens Of The World I would make it a law that every time guests were due for dinner, a recipe, brand new to the cook, would have to be tried. It has been my experience that cooks never wield their cooking fingers with better results than when tackling an exciting recipe for the first time. Ingredients get measured precisely. Sauces get stirred for the proper length of time. Results? A *perfectly* prepared whatever-it-is. There is no blurring of the beautifully balanced results because of carelessness inspired by overconfidence. Then too, there is the added enjoyment of experiencing, at the same time your guests do, the tasty concoction you have so carefully prepared. It's just like being a guest at your own party.

How to avoid last-minute-itis

Whenever you can prepare the initial stages of a recipe in advance, do so. If possible whip up the chosen dish in its entirety and set it aside until needed. Naturally this will not always be practical. I have marked with an asterisk the specific recipes that are easily prepared ahead of time, and have indicated just how far along they may be brought prior to serving without endangering their deliciousness. When it is necessary to do any last-minute cooking, always be sure the needed ingredients and equipment, serving dishes and spoons are neatly assembled and ready for instant action.

It takes a great deal of patience and planning to produce a dinner party that really comes off. The menu section of this book offers advice that applies to the esthetic aspects of choosing a menu. Under this, the practical section of the book, may I suggest another consideration in menu making? How to avoid last-minute-itis. Never choose more than one recipe that calls for a great deal of last-minute attention. Gear your menu, not only to good eating, but to the time you have available.

After years of experimenting I have found an almost foolproof system of serving a dinner for eight either unassisted or with one inexperienced helper.

If you have several in help or are in the habit of hiring specially trained help when you entertain, the limitations imposed by

your menu need not be so strict. You need only concern yourself with bringing the courses to be served up to the step prior
to serving, instructing the persons employed—either orally or
with detailed lists—and hoping no power struggles occur in the
kitchen, at least until after dessert.

However if you are, as I am, often forced to serve either alone
or with a neophyte helper, the following plan works wonderfully well.

THE DAY BEFORE THE DINNER PARTY

1. *Decide upon your menu, including the necessary
   wine or wines.*

   Select at least three hors d'oeuvres that can be prepared in
   their entirety either several hours or a day in advance of
   your party. Keep in refrigerator until needed.
   Eliminate soup course for a minimum amount of trouble.
   Pick a salad that can be ready to place on the table in individual plates when the hors d'oeuvre dishes are removed.

2. *Make a list of everything needed.*
3. *Do your shopping.*

THE DAY OF THE DINNER PARTY

1. *Midafternoon*

   Get the dining room ready for your guests.
   (a) Set the table for dinner no later than 2 o'clock in the
   afternoon.

(b) At the same time set up a sideboard or extra table with the serving plates and silver that will be needed.

(c) Close doors to dining room.

Cook dinner for children (something that can be popped into an oven set at any temperature, warmed, and served with a minimum amount of trouble).

Prepare the following as far as possible in advance.

(a) Soup

(b) Entrée

(c) Salad

(d) Vegetables

(e) Dessert

Wash utensils used in above.

Assemble and stack on one counter all ingredients and utensils needed to complete recipes.

2. *Early evening*

Give children dinner, hungry or not.

Take bath and get dressed. During bath make out instruction list for helper. (This is not easy if you are a shower-taker.)

Turn down children's beds, put out pajamas, give children any last-minute instructions.

3. *Just before guests arrive*

Complete whatever dishes will not be ruined by keeping warm until dinner.

Put ice in ice bucket and set out glasses on a tray.

Open wine.

4. *As the doorbell rings*

Wash hands.

Join husband and guests during predinner drinks.

5. *Just before dinner*

Place hors d'oeuvres on table.
If hot soup is to be served place on low flame.
Make salad.

6. *During dinner*

While hors d'oeuvres are being consumed have helper ladle
soup into soup plates. Tell her to wait 8 minutes after
everyone is seated.
After hors d'oeuvres assist helper in removing hors d'oeuvre
dishes.
Assist helper in serving soup.
If not serving soup, serve salad instead of soup after remov-
ing hors d'oeuvre dishes.
Instruct helper to remove soup plates and serve salad.
Meanwhile complete entrée and place vegetables in serving
dishes.
Assist helper in carrying entrée and vegetables to sideboard.
Instruct guests to serve themselves.
Meanwhile pour wine.
Enjoy dinner with your guests.
Helper should meanwhile have water boiling for coffee
and/or tea.
When your guests have been satisfied instruct helper to
remove all plates and food from table and sideboard.
Meanwhile set coffee and tea to brewing and complete
dessert.
If dessert is to be flamed before your admiring guests, carry
dessert to table, flame it, and serve.
Instruct helper to place cups and saucers beside your place
at the table.
Serve coffee.
When dessert is finished suggest a brandy in the living
room.

Exit guests, host, and hostess from dining room, closing
doors behind them to permit helper to work her magic
with the dirty dishes.
FINIS DINNER

Good grief! Here they come . . .

The most severe test in hostessing, or just plain homemaking
for that matter, is not the prearranged, preshopped, "dinner at
eight" kind of entertaining but rather the "Good grief! Here
they come up the front walk at meal time and I haven't a
thing in the house" kind of emergency cooking. A device I
employ to render this monstrous situation completely harm-
less is to have a checklist of ingredients tucked away in the
kitchen cupboard or the freezer ready to be transformed into
ambrosia at practically a moment's notice. Two things may be
accomplished by using this list:

1. A variety of menus may be prepared *in their entirety,* relying solely on the items here mentioned.
2. The remainder of recipes in this book may be prepared simply by purchasing several *main* ingredients, thus reducing shopping time and inconvenience to a bare minimum.

Naturally, it is not *necessary* to stock all the items mentioned
below, but the more of these gourmet aids that find a perma-
nent home in your kitchen, the more inclined you will be to
whip up something exotic when the occasion demands. Thus
your ascendance from a scrambled eggs cook to *Chef Formidable*
will be accelerated considerably merely by the purchase (over

a period of time if necessary) of the listed items. Please, don't let the length of the lists frighten you. The staple items you no doubt keep handy already, the spices take up very little room and last a long time, and the frozen foods, wines, cheeses, canned goods, hurry-ups, and gourmet staples, once purchased, may not need to be replaced for many, many months.

If you find you are missing many of the gourmet items in the following lists don't be discouraged. Merely add one or two of these interesting foods to your collection each week and soon your kitchen will be as intriguing as a magic shop and just as capable of producing magic.

STAPLE ITEMS

. . . Butter   . . . Pepper
. . . Flour   . . . Bacon
. . . Milk   . . . Cooking oil
. . . Sugar   . . . Mayonnaise
. . . Bread   . . . Spaghetti
. . . Eggs   . . . Minute rice
. . . Heavy cream   . . . Prepared mustard
. . . Onions   . . . Catsup
. . . Salt   . . . Honey

These staple items should be found in any well stocked kitchen. Mark how many you have in yours and check your score below:

(18) . . . *Your kitchen's a pleasure*   (10) . . . *Barely adequate*   (5) . . . *Your family is starving to death!*

SPICES AND HERBS

. . . Cinnamon   . . . Curry powder
. . . Cloves   . . . Fennel seed
. . . Parsley flakes . . . Tarragon
. . . Garlic powder   . . . Chervil

. . . Paprika
. . . Nutmeg
. . . Marjoram
. . . Thyme
. . . Dried mint leaves
. . . Orégano
. . . Dry mustard

. . . Basil
. . . Whole cloves
. . . Stick cinnamon
. . . Whole pepper
. . . Dill
. . . Sage

The spices on your shelf, like the lines in your palm, can tell more about you than you may suspect. Mark off the ones on *your* shelf and check your score below:

(21) . . . Why don't *you* write a cookbook?   (12) . . . You're a whiz!   (5) . . . You're off to a good start. Keep collecting!

GOURMET STAPLES

. . . Olive oil
. . . Croutons
. . . Anchovies
. . . Anchovy paste
. . . Bread crumbs
. . . Capers
. . . Chutney

. . . Shallots
. . . Wine vinegar
. . . Garlic (whole)
. . . Soy sauce
. . . Worcestershire sauce
. . . French dressing

These items show up more frequently in gourmet cooking than do the bread-and-milk type staples. How many do you consider indispensable?

(13) . . . Want to trade recipes?   (8) . . . Invite me to dinner!   (3) . . . You show promise—get out of that rut!

The following are hurry-up and substitute items not generally stocked. However, as they are relied upon most often in this book it would be a good idea never to be without them.

HURRY-UPS

Frozen green pepper, chopped* Lemon juice (bottled)†
Frozen raw onion, chopped* Frozen chopped chives

* Uncooked, chopped frozen green pepper and onion are readily available in the stores where I shop. You may find items available to you that are even better. Never hesitate to try new shortcuts you may discover at your store. If on the other hand you cannot find the above groceries at your food store, I would suggest you prepare and freeze your own so as always to have them handy.

To prepare: Wash and peel onions. Wash, remove seeds and cut green peppers into pieces. Dry both vegetables well. Chop into quarter-inch pieces and place on paper towels to remove moisture while you cover a cookie sheet with aluminum foil. Spread each vegetable on half of the covered cookie sheet. Cover vegetables with a second piece of aluminum foil, to keep odor from spreading through freezer. Freeze as quickly as possible. When frozen, scoop onion and green pepper quickly into separate plastic containers so as not to defrost. Store in freezer until needed.

† Although I find bottled, reconstituted lemon juice perfectly satisfactory as used in these recipes, if you feel strongly about using only "fresh" lemon juice, by all means squeeze your own. Add a minute or two more, however, to your cooking time.

CANNED GOODS

Beef consommé Tomato paste
Cream of chicken soup Pimento
Minced clams Mushrooms

FROZEN FOODS

Shrimp (Cooked and cleaned) Thin sliced rare roast beef
Mushrooms* Cooked lobster meat

* If not available at your food store be your own helper by cooking, freezing, and storing mushrooms in your freezer for future use. Wash

10 or 15 mushrooms and dry well with paper toweling. Melt ¼-pound stick of butter in skillet. Slowly cook mushrooms until they begin to look golden brown. Turn out flame and allow mushrooms to cool somewhat in the butter. When cool, place in plastic container with butter in pan. Freeze as quickly as possible. Keep solidly frozen until needed.

In addition, these wines and cheeses, used most often in gourmet cooking, are ideal to round out the perfectly stocked kitchen.

CHEESES

Blue Cheese	Grated Cheddar
Mozzarella	Grated Parmesan
Grated Swiss	

WINES, LIQUORS, LIQUEURS

Red wine (for cooking)	Sherry
White wine (for cooking)	Cognac

In addition a "neutral" red and a white wine and perhaps a rosé are nice to have on hand to dress up a spur-of-the-moment meal that must be planned when liquor stores are closed.

SPECIAL GOURMET ITEMS

If gourmet items such as truffles, pâté, etc., are not readily available in your area, do not despair. Most large department stores in bigger cities have gourmet departments and will be delighted to mail to you.

Reminder!

All recipes geared for two; simply double for four or add half a recipe more for each additional guest.

*Note starred recipes which can be prepared in advance, either completely or partially. Refer to footnotes for specific recommendations.

Hors d'oeuvres

Golden promises

Your guests have assembled. There has been the usual greeting, chatting, laughing and perhaps drinking. You've been there, enjoying the party as much as your guests, but now it's time to serve dinner. You slip into the kitchen where you have prepared every recipe, as far as was possible, in advance. You finish the preparation of the first course and lead your guests to the table.

Now! Your guests have been invited for dinner. This is perhaps the one moment in an evening that centers around dinner when the food has the complete attention of its audience. Conversations have been broken off, chairs have been settled. Your audience is in the palm of your hand. Don't just stand there. Enchant them!

Give them some luscious morsel that says, "See what you have in store?" Woo them with some tantalizing tidbit that cautions, "Don't blink an eye or you may miss something fantastic." Your guests are expectant. Lead them to expect even more. Through the hors d'oeuvres promise them the most delicious dinner they ever tasted, and then see that they're not disappointed.

MUSHROOMS STUFFED WITH WALNUTS AND PISTACHIOS GLAZED

If you are looking for a first course that is daringly different yet filled with flavors everyone will enjoy, sample this. Who could help but love mushrooms, walnuts, and pistachios hot and bubbling, with chutney? Don't hesitate to try it. It's really good.

INGREDIENTS

4 tablespoons butter
8 mushrooms, large
¼ cup pistachios, shelled
¼ cup walnuts
½ cup chutney

ASSEMBLE

1 skillet
1 paring knife
1 measuring cup
1 spoon
1 flameproof baking dish

DIRECTIONS

Light broiler. Set on high flame. Melt butter in skillet over medium flame. Peel mushrooms and chop stems. Add mushrooms to skillet and sauté for 2 minutes. Turn. Fry one minute more. Remove caps from pan. Measure chutney and add to butter in skillet. With paring knife chop any large pieces into pieces the size of your thumbnail. Add pistachios to skillet. Chop walnuts the same size as the chutney. Stir. Cook for one minute. Stuff mushrooms with mixture in the skillet. Serve hot.

GARNISH (*Optional*)

Top each mushroom with one small bit candied cherry and 2 green halves of pistachio nut set like a flower with 2 green leaves. Decorate plate with sprigs of watercress.

MOZZARELLA IN CARROZZA

This tasty little sautéed sandwich comes to the table all hot and golden and oozing with goodness in the form of Mozzarella cheese. Is it any wonder it is adored by epicures half the world round?

INGREDIENTS

8 thin slices white bread
8 tablespoons butter
2 tablespoons olive oil
4 thin slices Mozzarella cheese
8 strips anchovy paste
¾ cup fine bread crumbs
1 egg
1 tablespoon milk

ASSEMBLE

1 medium size skillet
1 set measuring spoons
1 cookie cutter or glass
1 fork or rotary beater
1 shallow bowl (for egg)
1 plate (for breadcrumbs)
1 sharp knife or cheese cutter

DIRECTIONS

Cut bread into rounds with cookie cutter. Place 4 tablespoons butter and 2 tablespoons olive oil in skillet to melt. Beat one egg and one tablespoon milk together in bowl. Butter one side of each slice of bread. Cut 4 slices Mozzarella cheese each ¼-inch thick. Place one slice cheese on every other buttered slice bread. Make an **x** of anchovy paste on every cheese slice. Top with another bread round with butter in center of sandwich. Dip Mozzarella sandwich in beaten egg, dip in bread crumbs, and fry in oil until golden, turning once.

GARNISH (*Optional*)

Place one rolled fillet of anchovy in the center of each serving of Mozzarella in Carrozza, and tuck a small piece of parsley on either side of this. Serve very hot.

RAMEKINS OF SHRIMP IN SOUR CREAM

Succulent shrimp and mushrooms in a rich, pink sour cream sauce. For a tempting opener to a very special meal you couldn't do better than this.

INGREDIENTS

8 large cooked and cleaned shrimp, available at your fish store
¾ cup sour cream
5 tablespoons butter
1 6-ounce package cooked and cleaned frozen mushrooms
¼ teaspoon salt
1 teaspoon Chinese soy sauce
2 teaspoons paprika
4 tablespoons grated Swiss cheese or Cheddar cheese, available in packages

ASSEMBLE

1 medium large skillet
1 measuring cup
1 tablespoon
1 set measuring spoons
1 small saucepan
2 large ramekins or individual fireproof casseroles

DIRECTIONS

Place the skillet over a medium flame and add to it the 5 tablespoons of butter. Add to this the frozen mushrooms and the shrimp. Turn the flame up to medium. Meanwhile heat the sour cream, the soy sauce, the paprika and the salt, in the small saucepan over low heat. Add the sour cream mixture to the shrimp and cook, stirring constantly for 2 minutes. Divide into ramekins and sprinkle with grated cheese. Place under broiler until cheese melts. Serve immediately.

COQUILLE ST. JACQUES*

A melt-in-your-mouth mixture of scallops, white wine, butter, and Parmesan cheese. A favorite first course of the French. Fix it and find out why.

INGREDIENTS

4 large scallops (uncooked)
1 3-ounce can mushrooms (chopped)
4 large mushrooms (fresh)
3 shallots
1 tablespoon white wine
2 tablespoons fine bread crumbs
2 teaspoons fine bread crumbs
2 teaspoons grated Parmesan cheese
3 tablespoons butter
1 tablespoon heavy cream
2 generous pinches of garlic powder

ASSEMBLE

1 food grinder
1 skillet
1 paring knife
1 set measuring spoons
paper toweling
2 large coquille shells for cooking and serving

DIRECTIONS

Turn broiler on high flame. Peel and wash shallots and fresh mushrooms. Drain on paper towels. Drain canned mushrooms. Put fresh mushrooms, shallots, scallops, and 2 tablespoons canned, chopped mushrooms through food grinder using fine blade. Meanwhile, melt 3 tablespoons butter in skillet. Add the ground materials, one tablespoon white wine, the remainder of the canned, chopped mushrooms, and 2 generous pinches garlic powder. Cook for 2 minutes over medium high heat, stirring constantly. Lower heat if mixture begins to stick to pan. Stir in one tablespoon heavy cream and 2 tablespoons bread crumbs. Turn off heat.*

When ready to serve heat coquille slightly in pan, then heap onto coquille shells. Sprinkle each with one teaspoon bread crumbs and one teaspoon Parmesan cheese. Place under broiler flame until slightly browned. Serve hot.

* May be prepared to this point 24 hours in advance and refrigerated until serving time.

FRESH MUSHROOMS IN DOUBLE CREAM

Never tried mushrooms raw? Better make amends to yourself and your guests by serving this pale and delicate perfection at the first possible opportunity. When uncooked, that perfect beauty the mushroom has a flavor and texture subtle in the extreme. Serve with White Bean and Anchovy Salad, Eggs À La Russe, and Onion Salad as one of a selection of French hors d'oeuvres.

INGREDIENTS
8 fresh mushrooms
1 cup sour cream
½ cup heavy sweet cream
12 drops Tabasco sauce

ASSEMBLE
1 paring knife
1 medium size mixing bowl
1 measuring cup
1 spoon
bowl for serving

DIRECTIONS

Peel mushrooms if necessary. Discard tough stems. Slice mushrooms into paper-thin slices. Mix one cup sour cream, ½ cup sweet cream, and 12 drops Tabasco sauce. Add mushrooms to the cream mixture and mix gently. Be careful not to break mushrooms. Place in serving bowl. Serve cold.

GARNISH

Sprinkle bowl with paprika. Decorate center of bowl with 4 mushroom slices (including stems).

ESCARGOTS IN CREAM

Snails dressed in a sauce that's different and delectable. A creamy, new way to serve this gourmet's delight.

INGREDIENTS

2 tablespoons butter
1½ teaspoons flour
½ small onion, chopped
½ cup heavy cream
2 egg yolks, thoroughly beaten
½ cup heavy cream
1 7½-ounce can snails, drained
salt and pepper to taste
4 toast points or prepared patty shells

ASSEMBLE

1 medium size skillet
1 set measuring spoons
1 sharp knife
1 can opener
1 strainer
1 measuring cup
1 small saucepan
1 tablespoon
1 mixing bowl
1 fork or rotary beater
2 small serving plates

DIRECTIONS

Put skillet on low flame. Add 2 tablespoons butter. Add 1½ teaspoons flour. Stir. Peel and chop finely ½ of a small onion. Add to butter in skillet. Meanwhile drain snails in strainer and add to the butter-flour mixture. In saucepan heat ½ cup cream to boiling but do not boil! Add to the skillet. Stir well and simmer gently while you beat the 2 egg yolks in a mixing bowl. Add the other ½ cup of cream to the beaten egg yolks and mix thoroughly. Pour the egg-cream mixture into the skillet and cook over low fire, stirring constantly until thickened. Do not let mixture boil or egg yolks will curdle. Add salt and white pepper to taste. Serve steaming hot in hot patty shells or on toast points.

GARNISH (*Optional*)

Tuck tiny pieces of parsley around the edge of the serving dishes. Sprinkle with nutmeg. Serve hot.

FRESH VEGETABLES WITH TUNA DIP*

Crisp scallions, radishes, and carrot sticks, juicy cherry tomatoes arranged around a "dunk" whose goodness no one will be able to decipher. The secret ingredient? Tuna fish. Served at one of New York's favorite French restaurants as a between-course treat, it makes a wonderful something to serve with drinks.

INGREDIENTS	ASSEMBLE
2 large carrots	1 potato peeler
8 scallions	1 blender
10 radishes	1 paring knife
16 cherry tomatoes	1 set measuring spoons
½ 3¼-ounce can tuna	1 mixing bowl
2 tablespoons milk	1 serving plate with attached
2 tablespoons mayonnaise	bowl for dip
½ cup sour cream	
2 tablespoons heavy cream	
1 small onion	

DIRECTIONS

Wash carrots, scallions, radishes, and cherry tomatoes. Do not remove green stems from tomatoes or radishes. Peel carrots with potato peeler to remove skin. Cut into strips ½ inch wide and 3 inches long. Cut roots from scallions and radishes. Plunge all vegetables into icy water and refrigerate until needed. Open tuna fish and drain. Put ¼ can tuna, 2 tablespoons milk, 2 tablespoons mayonnaise, 1 small onion peeled and chopped, and ½ cup sour cream into blender. Blend 1½ minutes. Add 2 tablespoons heavy cream. Mix. When ready to serve place tuna dip in dip container of serving dish. Drain vegetables and arrange attractively on the plate. Serve cold.

GARNISH (*Optional*)

Decorate top of dip with a design of flowers and leaves cut from carrots, radishes, and scallion greens. Surround dip with vegetables.

NOTE

To serve 4, double quantity of vegetables only.

* May be prepared several hours in advance of serving. Refrigerate until needed.

ITALIAN ANTIPASTO*

Here's a delightful way to begin an Italian meal, or almost any other. Even the most stubborn appetite can't resist so many tempting tidbits. Better do as the Italians do and whip one up for dinner tonight.

INGREDIENTS

1 3½-ounce can tuna fish
4 anchovy fillets
1 green pepper
1 tomato
6 slices canned beets (cold)
8 strips of pimento
8 black olives
8 green olives
2 thin slices Provolone cheese
2 slices Italian salami
4 scallions
6 cold cooked shrimp, available
   at your fish store
¼ cup olive oil
2 or 3 tablespoons wine vinegar
4 leaves lettuce

ASSEMBLE

1 can opener
1 colander
paper toweling
1 paring knife
1 large serving plate

DIRECTIONS

Wash green pepper, tomato, 4 scallions, and 4 leaves lettuce. Drain on paper toweling. Open cans of tuna fish and beets. Drain beets in colander. Arrange lettuce to cover serving platter. Drain oil from tuna fish by holding can of tuna (with lid) upside down and pressing lid against fish. Turn whole can of tuna in center of serving plate. Drain 4 fillets of anchovies on paper toweling. Slice tomato. Remove stem and pulp from green pepper. Slice into one-inch strips. Arrange anchovy fillets, tomato slices, green pepper strips, scallions, pimento strips, cheese, and salami slices attractively around the plate. Garnish with shrimps, olives, and beet slices. Dribble ¼ cup oil and 3 tablespoons wine vinegar over everything but the tuna fish. Serve cold.

* May be prepared one or two hours in advance. Follow recipe up to point where olive oil and wine vinegar are added. Refrigerate. Continue recipe several minutes before serving.

TARTAR SANDWICHES

Looking for something hearty to serve with drinks? These tasty raw steak sandwiches are sure to be a hit— especially with the men.

INGREDIENTS

½ pound ground steak. Ask your butcher to put it through the grinder that has not been used for pork.

1 sweet onion, finely chopped

4 small slices rye bread

1 egg yolk

8 thin anchovy fillets

2 stuffed olives

44 capers

ASSEMBLE

1 paring knife

1 small bowl or cup for egg yolk

1 fork

1 pastry brush

paper toweling

serving plate

DIRECTIONS

Peel, wash, and chop onion. Blot 8 anchovy fillets on paper toweling. Spread bread with chopped meat. Beat egg yolk with fork. Brush outer one inch of meat with egg yolk. Criss-cross tartar sandwich with anchovy fillets. Press chopped onion into egg-brushed meat. Decorate raw meat with 10 capers per sandwich. Slice olives. Put 1 slice olive where anchovy fillets cross. Place 1 caper in the center of each olive slice. Serve cold.

FRESH FIGS AND WALNUTS IN PROSCIUTTO HAM CONES*

Another opener that comes to us from Italy. Fresh figs rolled in walnuts and wrapped in thin slices of pink prosciutto. A beautiful start to even the most delicate meal.

INGREDIENTS

4 fresh figs
4 large slices of prosciutto
10 sprigs watercress
1 egg white
¼ cup walnut meats, finely chopped

ASSEMBLE

1 paring knife
1 fork
1 small plate
1 small bowl
paper toweling
pastry brush
2 small serving plates

DIRECTIONS

Wash the watercress and trim any tough stems. Wash figs. Dry both on paper toweling. Arrange watercress on serving plates. Roll the prosciutto on the diagonal with one end closed and one end open, to form a cornucopia or cone. Place egg white in small bowl. Beat with fork. Brush fig lightly with egg white. Roll in nut meats. Insert the ripe fig in prosciutto cone. Place on the bed of watercress. Serve cold.

NOTE

To serve 4, double all ingredients but egg white.

* May be prepared an hour or two in advance of serving.

Soups supreme
Hot and cold

Soup is the most maligned member of all the courses in the family of foods. And the most wonderful! Anyone who calls soup dull, ordinary, unglamorous, or any other ugly-duckling name will have to fight with me. Beautiful soup would be more like it. Warm soup. Comforting soup. Even clever soup. Wise soup. Magic soup. What other food is almost always served in the same form—liquid—and yet manages to conceal within its sameness such differences of taste? Such subtleties of taste transformed from turnips or carrots or lemons or cabbages into liquids. Disguised. Hidden like secrets in the depths of the bowl. Secrets willing to be discovered if the sipper will but take the time. Puzzles created over hundreds of years. Ancient Greek puzzles, squeezed into a bowl and waiting to be puzzled out. Sometimes complex. Sometimes so simple that only a drop of this or a sprinkle of that can make the difference. Sip, don't gulp. This is the languid spot in the meal. The teaser after the invitation, the promise of the hors d'oeuvre. It should be a combination of tastes that lead away from the first course and into the main course, usually with a little something of both hidden in it. Sip, don't gulp. Walk, don't run to the nearest main course. And while you're here . . . enjoy it.

CURRIED LEMON SOUP*

One of the most beautiful soups in the world! From the soft yellow color to the lovely lemon flavor, this soup does what it sets out to do—be lovely, be cool, be impressive, be delicious!

INGREDIENTS

1 10½-ounce can cream of chicken soup
1 cup light cream
3 tablespoons prepared lemon juice
2 teaspoons curry powder
1 tablespoon water

ASSEMBLE

1 can opener
1 measuring cup
1 blender
1 set measuring spoons
1 spoon
1 paring knife
2 soup plates

DIRECTIONS

Open one can of chicken soup and pour into blender. Measure one cup of cream. Pour into blender. Put tablespoon of water into cup. Measure 2 teaspoons curry powder. Add to water in measuring cup. Stir. Add to mixture in blender. Cover. Blend at high speed for one minute. Measure 3 tablespoons lemon juice. Stir into soup.* Pour soup into bowls. Serve extremely cold.

GARNISH (*Optional*)

Slice two thin slices of lemon. Top each slice with one blanched almond with tiny mint leaves on either side.

* If preparing in advance, omit lemon until immediately before garnishing. Garnish immediately before serving.

REAL FRENCH ONION SOUP*

This is it—practically the national dish of France and the heart's delight of Francophiles everywhere. Real savory, golden brown onion soup guaranteed to make your guests say "The best I ever tasted" now yours to make in mere minutes. Bon appetit!

INGREDIENTS

2 small onions, or one medium sized one
3 tablespoons butter
1 tablespoon flour
1 10½-ounce can beef consommé
½ soup can water
2 slices French bread
¼ teaspoon garlic powder
1 tablespoon olive oil
6 tablespoons grated Swiss cheese

ASSEMBLE

1 skillet (medium size)
1 skillet (small)
1 paring knife
1 set measuring spoons
1 fork for stirring
1 can opener
2 individual flameproof soup servers

DIRECTIONS

Melt 2 tablespoons of butter in a medium size skillet. Peel 2 onions and slice thinly. Sauté onions in 2 tablespoons of butter over medium high heat until the onions are soft. Stir occasionally to keep from browning. Sprinkle with one tablespoon flour, and stir. Add one can consommé and one half can of water. Stir and bring to a boil. Boil for one minute. Meanwhile heat the remaining tablespoon butter, the tablespoon of olive oil, and ¼ teaspoon garlic powder in the small skillet. Cut 2 slices of French bread and fry them in this mixture. Place bread in bottom of serving bowl. Divide the hot onion soup evenly between the two soup servers. Sprinkle each with 3 tablespoons grated Swiss Cheese and serve immediately.

* If preparing in advance reserve garlic bread slices and omit Swiss cheese. Refrigerate until shortly before serving time. Several minutes before time to serve, heat onion soup mixture and continue recipe.

CREAM OF ASPARAGUS SOUP WITH ASPARAGUS TIPS AND ANCHOVY CROUTONS

You won't believe asparagus soup can taste so good until you try this for yourself. The mellow flavor of creamed asparagus is superbly set off by spicy anchovy croutons. And the treasure in the bottom of the bowl? Asparagus of course.

INGREDIENTS

1 10½-ounce can cream of asparagus soup
½ cup heavy cream
8 canned asparagus tips
2 slices bread, preferably two
   days old
4 tablespoons butter
2 teaspoons anchovy paste
⅛ teaspoon garlic powder

ASSEMBLE

1 saucepan
1 measuring cup
1 can opener
1 paring knife
1 set measuring spoons
1 skillet
1 rotary beater
2 soup plates

DIRECTIONS

Mix together with rotary beater one can cream of asparagus soup and ½ cup heavy cream. If thinner soup is preferred, add a small amount of milk. Place on low heat. Open can of asparagus tips. Drain. Place 8 tips in the saucepan with the soup. Meanwhile cut the crusts from 2 slices of bread. Spread bread with 2 teaspoons anchovy paste. Cut bread into one-inch squares. Melt butter in skillet. Add ⅛ teaspoon garlic powder. Fry bread cubes in the butter until they are golden. Carefully pour the asparagus soup into the 2 serving bowls. Place 4 asparagus tips in the bottom of each bowl. Be careful to keep the tips whole. Place anchovy croutons in a small bowl and spoon into soup at table. Serve hot.

POTATO-CORN CLAM CHOWDER

If there is a soup more hearty or delicious than clam chowder it is Potato-Corn Clam Chowder. This is perfect when served with a New England dinner or on its own as a wonderfully warming lunch.

INGREDIENTS

½ 10½-ounce can cream of potato soup
½ 8-ounce can creamed corn
½ 7½-ounce can minced clams
2 slices bacon
½ cup light cream
½ cup milk
⅛ teaspoon garlic powder
2 tablespoons butter
a dash or two of paprika

ASSEMBLE

1 medium size saucepan
1 can opener
1 paring knife
1 set measuring spoons
2 soup plates

DIRECTIONS

Cut 2 bacon strips into quarters. Place in bottom of saucepan. Fry over medium heat until cooked but not crisp. Remove from flame. Add ½ can cream of potato soup, ½ can creamed corn, ½ can minced clams to pan. Spoon clams in carefully so as not to disturb any sand there might be in the bottom of the can. Add ½ cup light cream, ½ cup milk, and ⅛ teaspoon garlic powder to pan. Stir. Cook over medium heat until scalding but not boiling. Ladle soup into soup plates. Top each bowl with one tablespoon butter and a dash of paprika. Serve immediately.

NOTE

Serves 2 or 3.

JELLIED MADRILENE IN AVOCADO SHELLS

More than an hors d'oeuvre, more than a soup, this dish can very easily take the place of both. See what a nice start it is for a simple luncheon or for a cold dish dinner. Easy cooking has never been more tasty!

INGREDIENTS

1 avocado
1 12½-ounce can jellied Madrilene, chilled
2 teaspoons chilled French dressing
16 drops lemon juice
2 heaping tablespoons sour cream
2 teaspoons dried crushed mint leaves, or fresh mint chopped fine
4 fresh mint leaves, if available

ASSEMBLE

1 paring knife
1 can opener
1 tablespoon
1 set measuring spoons
2 serving plates

DIRECTIONS

Cut avocado in half lengthwise. Carefully take out seed and pull off peel. If in a super-hurry, avocado may be left unpeeled. Place one teaspoon French dressing in each avocado shell. Open one can of jellied madrilene. Stir once with tablespoon. Immediately heap jellied madrilene into the hollows of the avocados. Sprinkle each with 8 drops prepared lemon juice.

GARNISH

Top each jellied madrilene with one tablespoon of sour cream. Serve very cold. Sprinkle each with one teaspoon dried mint leaves. Top each with two mint leaves placed on the dollop of sour cream.

GAZPACHO*

Looking for a soup that's cool, delectable, and a show-stopper as well? Stop here. Gazpacho's your dish. Serve frosty bowls of tomato-beef broth with mounds of chopped, fresh vegetables for your guests to add as they wish. It's a beautiful soup both to see and to eat. Eat some and see.

INGREDIENTS

1 large tomato
1 medium size cucumber
½ cup chopped green pepper, frozen, uncooked
5 scallions
3 small cloves garlic
1 cup cold tomato juice
1 cup cold consommé
4 tablespoons olive oil
¼ teaspoon salt
3 tablespoons prepared lemon juice
6 drops Tabasco sauce
¼ cup fine bread crumbs
2 ice cubes

ASSEMBLE

1 blender (if not available mix with rotary beater)
1 paring knife
1 measuring cup
1 set measuring spoons
1 garlic press
1 set of small bowls
2 soup plates

DIRECTIONS

Place in blender one cup cold tomato juice, one cup cold consommé, ¼ cup bread crumbs, 6 drops Tabasco sauce, 4 tablespoons olive oil, ¼ teaspoon salt, and 3 tablespoons lemon juice. Peel 3 cloves garlic and add to blender. Cover blender. Turn on high speed for one minute. Meanwhile, wash one tomato and 5 scallions. Peel one cucumber. Chop tomato, cucumber, and scallions the size of your thumbnail. Place vegetables in individual bowls.* Place ice cubes in serving bowls. Pour mixture in blender over ice cubes. Remove ice cubes. Serve immediately. Have guests help themselves to the raw vegetables which they may place in the bowl with the soup.

GARNISH (*Optional*)

Top each bowl of soup with 1 tablespoon finely chopped parsley and one very thin slice unpeeled cucumber.

* May be prepared several hours in advance of serving. Place in refrigerator until serving time. Blend slightly before using.

CHILLY CREME DE MENTHE SOUP

A soup fascinating in its unusual flavor. Smoky and minty at the same time, thinly creamy, deliciously cool. "Odd-ball" but definitely worth a try.

INGREDIENTS

⅓ 11-ounce can split green pea soup (with ham)
⅓ 10½-ounce can cream of celery soup
⅓ 10½-ounce can cream of chicken soup
1 cup of light cream
a pinch of garlic powder
a pinch of thyme
1 teaspoon parsley flakes
3 tablespoons water
2 tablespoons crème de menthe
3 ice cubes

ASSEMBLE

1 blender (if not available mix soup in a bowl and strain)
1 measuring cup
1 tablespoon
1 set measuring spoons
2 soup plates

DIRECTIONS

Place ⅓ can each pea soup, cream of chicken soup, and cream of celery soup in blender with a pinch each of thyme and garlic powder, plus 3 ice cubes, cracked. Add one teaspoon parsley flakes and 3 tablespoons water. Blend on high speed for one minute. Turn off blender. Add one cup light cream to blender mixture. Blend on low for 10 seconds more. Add 2 tablespoons crème de menthe. Blend on low speed for 10 seconds. Pour into soup plates. Serve cold.

May also be served without crème de menthe, either hot or cold.

GARNISH (*Optional*)

Serve with a dollop of whipped cream in the center of the soup. Tuck 3 fresh mint leaves slightly under the whipped cream. Serve immediately.

GARLIC SOUP WITH CROUTONS AND POACHED EGG*

Soupophiles, be sure to try this epicure's delight. Steaming, garlicky beef broth, tender poached egg, and garlic croutons surely make this a treat in itself as well as a harbinger of good things to come.

INGREDIENTS

4 tablespoons good olive oil
1 teaspoon garlic powder
20 ready-made croutons or bread cubes
1 10½-ounce can consommé
¾ soup can water
2 eggs
2 thin slices tomato
dash each salt, pepper, and paprika

ASSEMBLE

1 large skillet
1 set measuring spoons
1 can opener
1 slotted spoon
1 paring knife
1 fine strainer
2 soup plates

DIRECTIONS

Place the skillet over medium heat. Add 4 tablespoons olive oil and one teaspoon garlic powder. Add croutons or bread cubes and fry for one minute. Turn often. Remove croutons from pan with slotted spoon. Add one can consommé, ¾ can of water, and one dash of paprika to pan. Bring to a boil. When boiling turn flame down until liquid is barely bubbling. Break eggs into liquid. Be careful not to break yolks. Spoon liquid over eggs until they are cooked (about 3 minutes). Remove eggs with slotted spoon carefully and place one in each serving dish. Strain consommé into bowls over eggs. Sprinkle with salt, pepper, and paprika. Add croutons and tomato slices. Serve instantly.

GARNISH (*Optional*)
Sprinkle with finely chopped fresh parsley before serving.

* To prepare in advance make croutons and keep at room temperature. Make soup and refrigerate. Shortly before serving heat soup to steaming, add eggs, and continue as above.

TOMATO CRAB BISQUE

If there were only one soup in the whole world, all would be well if it was Tomato Crab Bisque. Pale tomato in color, delicately textured, it's replete with the can't-be-forgotten flavor of crab meat and sherry. Serve only for V.I.P.'s—and for yourself, of course.

INGREDIENTS

½ 10¾-ounce can cream of tomato soup
½ 10½-ounce can beef con-
   sommé
½ 11¼-ounce can split pea soup
   (without ham)
¼ pint light cream
¼ cup sherry
¼ pound crab meat (frozen)

ASSEMBLE

1 large saucepan
1 rotary beater
1 tablespoon
1 measuring cup
1 can opener
2 soup plates

DIRECTIONS

Mix the soups together in the saucepan. Use no water. Add ¼ pint cream and beat with the rotary beater until mixed. Remove shells from ¼ pound crab meat by picking through it with fingers and discarding anything that feels hard. Put the crab meat in the soup mixture and heat until steaming. Do not boil. Add ¼ cup sherry, a little at a time. Ladle into serving bowls. Serve hot.

GARNISH (*Optional*)

Chop 2 tablespoons parsley and sprinkle over center of soup. Sprinkle the outer edges of the soup with paprika. Serve hot.

The entrée
Supreme moment of the meal

As elegant and enticing as your hors d'oeuvre has been, as soothing and full of promise as has been your soup, still these have been but a prologue leading to the main attraction, the entrée. Thus far in your meal you have hinted at what was to come—made beautiful promises. Now the time has arrived to make those promises good. The main course must live up to the expectations of your guests, magic *you* have led them to expect by the perfection of your first two courses.

Does that sound like a challenge? It is! But one you can handle with ease. There is nothing chance about a perfect meal. It must be planned and executed with care. Quick does not mean haphazard! A meal should be planned with the entrée as its peak. Choose your main course first, then build out on either side. Pick up a spice in your main event and repeat it, subtly, in your soup. Isolate a texture or a flavor or even a color and extend it in a way complementary to your entrée.

It's just a matter of *thinking* about your foods as the individual personalities that they are. Select your foods as carefully as you select your friends and vice versa, and your reputation as a cook will soar as well as your reputation as a hostess.

SHRIMPS FLAMBÉ

Shrimps with a flourish! Exciting to look at, even more exciting to eat, and what oohs and aahs when you perform your cookery right at the table!

INGREDIENTS	ASSEMBLE
16 very large cleaned, uncooked shrimp, available at your fish store	1 chafing dish Sterno
½ teaspoon garlic powder	1 tablespoon
5 tablespoons butter	1 set measuring spoons
¼ cup applejack or apple brandy	1 measuring cup
¼ cup heavy cream	1 small saucepan
¼ teaspoon nutmeg	
1 tablespoon frozen chopped chives	

DIRECTIONS

Light flame under blazer pan of chafing dish. Melt 5 tablespoons butter. Add shrimp and garlic powder. Cook over high heat for 3 minutes. Remove from flame. Gently heat the applejack in the small saucepan. Pour gently over shrimps and light with a match. When brandy burns out, cook over high flame for 2 minutes. Add cream and nutmeg. Stir until hot. Sprinkle with chopped chives. Serve hot, either alone or over toast points or rice.

NOTE

This entire process may be performed at the table or, if desired, while still in kitchen bring recipe to point where brandy is added and continue from this point before guests.

WINE

Pouilly-Fuissé, slightly chilled

BOUILLABAISSE

A zesty and potent dark golden fish stew—An humble soup glorified by gourmets the world round—A fisherman's offspring turned king of the table, boullabaisse reigns as the world's favorite fish dish.

INGREDIENTS

1 whole cooked lobster in shell, cut in 1-inch pieces
14 frozen shrimp, cleaned and shelled
1 3¾-ounce can king crab meat
¼ pound fillet of flounder
¼ pound tail end of cod
¼ pound red snapper
¼ pound eel
If any of the above are not available, replace with a similar variety of fish
½ cup frozen or canned chopped carrot
½ cup frozen chopped onion
6 tablespoons tomato sauce or 3 tablespoons tomato paste
1 teaspoon garlic powder
2 teaspoons dried parsley
½ teaspoon fennel seeds
½ teaspoon thyme
2 small bay leaves
1½ teaspoon saffron
2 tablespoons frozen concentrated orange juice
1 teaspoon instant coffee

ASSEMBLE

1 large pot
1 tablespoon
1 nut cracker
1 sharp knife
1 cooking spoon
paper toweling
1 can opener
1 set measuring spoons
2 soup plates

1 10½-ounce can consommé
½ soup can clam juice
1 teaspoon anchovy paste
¼ cup olive oil
2 slices prepared garlic bread,
   frozen

DIRECTIONS

Place one can consommé and ½ can clam juice in pot. Cook over hot fire. Add 6 tablespoons tomato sauce or 3 tablespoons tomato paste, one teaspoon garlic powder, 2 teaspoons dried parsley, ½ teaspoon fennel seeds, ½ teaspoon thyme, 2 small bay leaves, 1½ teaspoons saffron, 2 tablespoons frozen orange juice concentrate, one teaspoon instant coffee, one teaspoon anchovy paste, and ¼ cup olive oil. Continue to boil while you cut fish into ¾-inch slices. Place fish slices in pot. Add frozen shrimp. Remove claws from lobster. Crack slightly with nut cracker. Cut lobster, shell and all, into one-inch slices. Add lobster and claws to pot. Place flounder pieces on top of boiling soup. Drain crab meat. Add to pot. Boil rapidly for 4 minutes. Meanwhile heat 2 pieces frozen garlic bread in skillet. Place garlic bread in soup plate. Ladle soup and fish over bread. Serve hot.

WINE
Pouilly-Fuissé slightly chilled

FISH WITH BEER AND GINGER SNAPS

If you're looking for a main course that is different to the point of being adventurous, serve this! Luscious white fish swimming in a sauce made from sparkling dark beer, with its flavor sweetened and heightened with ginger snaps. Not everyone's plate of fish, but definitely a winner for that guest who is always eager to try something exciting and new.

INGREDIENTS	ASSEMBLE
2 fillets of flounder	1 large skillet
¼ teaspoon salt	1 set measuring spoons
½ teaspoon lemon juice	1 paring knife
1 bay leaf	1 measuring cup
3 ginger snaps	1 spoon
¼ teaspoon sugar	1 small mixing bowl
1 tablespoon butter	paper toweling
1½ teaspoons flour	
1 cup dark beer	

DIRECTIONS

Wash fish. Sprinkle with ¼ teaspoon salt. To measure beer allow foam to settle slightly. Place one cup dark beer, one bay leaf, and the fish in the skillet with ½ teaspoon lemon juice. Add ¼ teaspoon sugar. Turn on medium high heat. If fish begins to break up, reduce flame to rather low. Meanwhile, remove 4 tablespoons of the fish-beer liquid, and place in mixing bowl with 3 ginger snaps. Add 1½ teaspoons flour and one tablespoon butter to this. Mash with spoon until fairly smooth. Remove fish from liquid and keep warm. Add mixture in mixing bowl to that in the skillet. Cook over high heat until slightly thickened. Pour several tablespoonfuls over fish. Serve hot.

ᴳᴬ ʀ ɴ ɪ s ʜ (*Optional*)

Serve with 2 sprigs of parsley under 2 thin slices of lemon. Top lemon with small criss-cross of pimento slices. Serve immediately.

ᴡ ɪ ɴ ᴇ

Rhine (4), German Dry, slightly chilled

SHRIMP CURRY

Here's a heavenly curry cooked with coconut milk for a taste surprise. Different but divine and a real reputation builder too!

INGREDIENTS

16 large cooked and cleaned shrimp, available at your fish store
1 4-ounce can shredded coconut
2½ cups milk
2 tablespoons flour
1 teaspoon salt
1½ tablespoons curry powder
3 tablespoons butter

ASSEMBLE

2 saucepans (6 cup)
1 skillet
1 strainer
2 spoons
1 colander
1 measuring cup
measuring spoons

DIRECTIONS

Put the shredded coconut and the milk into one saucepan. Heat until scalding but do not boil. In the other pan place the shrimps and 2 cups of hot water. Let stand until shrimps are hot. Meanwhile, melt butter in frying pan. Add salt and flour and stir until smooth. Add the curry powder and again stir until smooth.

Use the strainer to drain the milk from the coconut. Retain both. Pour milk into butter and flour mixture. Stir constantly over medium high flame until this begins to bubble and thicken. Cook for one minute more. Drain shrimp in colander. Pour curry sauce into serving bowl. Decorate with shrimp and shredded coconut. Serve hot with rice.

NOTE

This recipe serves 2 generously. To serve 3 add 8 large shrimp *only*. To serve 4 double entire recipe.

WINE

Bordeaux Graves, slightly chilled

ESCARGOTS BOURGUIGNONNE
(Snails Burgundy)

Succulent snails in the traditional garlic sauce—the classic of French gourmet cooking ready to delight your guests in mere minutes! Fabulous for that really special occasion.

INGREDIENTS

1 7½-ounce can snails with package of snail shells
5 tablespoons cognac
¼ teaspoon garlic powder
¼ teaspoon salt
¼ pound butter
1 teaspoon garlic powder
2 tablespoons dried parsley leaves
2 tablespoons frozen chopped chives, or fresh chives chopped

ASSEMBLE

1 can opener
1 set measuring spoons
1 strainer
1 small pan
2 tablespoons
dish towel
mixing bowl
flat flameproof dish or pan

DIRECTIONS

Light broiler and set on high. Drain one can snails in strainer. Put pan on stove and add 5 tablespoons of cognac, ¼ teaspoon garlic powder, ¼ teaspoon salt, and drained snails. Heat over medium high flame. Meanwhile in the mixing bowl mash with a spoon ¼-pound cold butter. Add one teaspoon of garlic powder, 2 tablespoons dried parsley leaves, 2 tablespoons chopped chives, and mix thoroughly with the cold butter. Place ¼ teaspoon of butter mixture in each of the snail shells. Drain the snails again in strainer. Add one snail to each of the snail shells. Use the rest of the butter mixture to seal the openings of the snail shells. Place the filled snail shells on the flat flame-proof dish or pan. Heat under the broiler for 3 minutes. Serve very hot.

WINE
Bordeaux Graves, slightly chilled

SHRIMP SCAMPI

You'll never believe this old gourmet standby is so easy to come up with! Large succulent shrimp swimming in sputtering hot garlic-butter sauce—a real winner any time.

INGREDIENTS

14 very large shrimp or prawns, raw
¼ cup olive oil
3 tablespoons butter
¼ teaspoon salt
3 cloves garlic
1 tablespoon parsley flakes

ASSEMBLE

1 pair scissors
paper toweling
1 garlic press
1 measuring cup
1 set measuring spoons
1 skillet
2 serving plates

DIRECTIONS

Remove shell from shrimp and clean by making a ¼-inch cut with scissors down the middle of the round back of the shrimp. Remove the vein down center of back. Wash in cold water and place each shrimp, as it is cleaned, on paper toweling to drain. Place skillet over high flame. Add ¼ cup olive oil and 3 tablespoons butter. Add shrimp. Cook shrimp about 3 minutes. Stir often. Crush garlic cloves over shrimp. Add garlic pulp to contents of skillet with parsley and salt. Cook for one minute more. Stir several times. Place seven shrimp on each plate. Divide sauce evenly. Serve very hot.

WINE

Pouilly-Fuissé, slightly chilled

DANISH FISH WITH BLUE CHEESE

Pearly white halibut in a lusciously piquant blue cheese sauce. A gourmet's delight and so amazingly easy to prepare.

INGREDIENTS

2 slices fresh halibut, not too thick
⅛ pound butter
½ cup Danish blue cheese
½ teaspoon salt
1 tablespoon lemon juice
2 wedges of lemon
2 sprigs parsley

ASSEMBLE

paper toweling
1 skillet
1 tablespoon
1 paring knife
1 set measuring spoons
1 fork
1 flameproof dish for broiling and serving

DIRECTIONS

Turn broiler flame on high. Wash fish. Blot with paper toweling. Rub fish with ½ teaspoon salt. Place several small pieces of butter in the broiling dish. Place fish in broiling dish. Put under broiler flame. In the skillet melt the remaining butter. Stir in ½ cup blue cheese and one tablespoon lemon juice. Baste fish with this mixture. Continue cooking until fish flakes when pricked with a fork, or about 7 minutes. Decorate fish with lemon wedges and sprigs of parsley. Serve hot.

WINE

Pouilly-Fuissé, slightly chilled

CALF'S LIVER PARIS

Have you been convinced for years that there is only one way to fix liver and that is fried with bacon? Then this recipe should be a revelation to you. Thin slices of that lovely liver, perfectly combined with shallots, nutmeg, and white wine—and not a slice of bacon in sight. Leave it to the Parisiennes.

INGREDIENTS

4 very thin slices of calf's liver
6 tablespoons butter
4 whole shallots
¾ cup dry white wine
1 tablespoon lemon juice
1 egg yolk
2 large pinches of salt
4 sprigs parsley
1 pinch nutmeg

ASSEMBLE

1 large skillet
1 medium size skillet
1 set measuring spoons
1 measuring cup
1 paring knife
1 fork
paper toweling
1 serving plate

DIRECTIONS

Wash liver slices and blot with paper toweling. Melt butter in medium sized skillet. Peel, wash, and chop shallots. Add to butter in pan. Cook for one minute over high flame. Add the wine and the nutmeg, and continue to cook over high heat for 2 minutes more. Add the lemon juice and turn flame very low. Wash and chop parsley. In large skillet quickly sear the liver slices on both sides over high heat. Remove from pan and keep warm. Beat egg yolk and add to sauce with salt. Stir until slightly thickened. Place the liver slices on serving dish and cover with the sauce. Sprinkle with chopped parsley and serve immediately.

GARNISH (*Optional*)

Place 5 or 6 cherry tomatoes in skillet with 2 tablespoons butter. Cook over medium heat for a few minutes. Arrange cherry tomatoes a few inches apart around edge of dish. Tuck whole parsley leaves beside each tomato. Serve hot.

WINE

Beaujolais

BREAST OF CHICKEN IN RUM CRUMBS

A warm buttery delight! A crusty "sandwich" where chicken slices sautéed in rum crumbs are the "bread" and marrons and chutney form the filling.

INGREDIENTS

2 chicken breasts, boneless
½ cup fine bread crumbs
¼ cup rum
1 tablespoon rum
1 tablespoon chutney, with liquid
3 marrons glacès
¼ pound butter

ASSEMBLE

1 small saucepan
1 sharp knife
1 large skillet
1 measuring cup
1 mallet or meat tenderizer
1 fork
1 small bowl
1 plate (for breadcrumbs)
serving plate

DIRECTIONS

Pull skin from chicken. Flatten each half chicken breast slightly with mallet or fine side of meat tenderizer. Place bread crumbs on plate. Pour ¼ cup rum into small bowl. Dip chicken in rum, then in bread crumbs. Turn flame medium high. Melt butter in skillet. Sauté each chicken slice one minute on each side or until golden. Meanwhile, mash marrons and chutney with one tablespoon rum. Warm in saucepan. Add a few bread crumbs if needed to make mixture spreadable. Spread this on one side of 2 chicken slices. Top with another sautéed chicken slice. Serve hot.

GARNISH

See recipe for Marrons in Apricots. Tuck one small piece of parsley under each apricot half. Serve hot.

WINE

Beaujolais or Bordeaux Graves, slightly chilled

LOBSTER-SHRIMP OR CRAYFISH IN WINE RICE

One of the most delicate dishes. Bright red-orange lobster-shrimp or crayfish steeped in the most subtle of subtle sauces. Don't say wine and rice don't mix well until you've tasted this for yourself.

INGREDIENTS	ASSEMBLE
10 lobster-shrimp or crayfish	1 scissors
6 tablespoons butter	1 medium size saucepan
1 tablespoon brandy	1 large skillet
1 bay leaf	1 set measuring spoons
large pinch of thyme	1 measuring cup
4 shallots	1 colander
2 tablespoons chopped parsley	1 paring knife
1 cup dry white wine	paper toweling
2 tablespoons tomato sauce	1 serving dish
6 tablespoons cream	
1 cup minute rice	
¼ teaspoon salt	

DIRECTIONS

Prepare minute rice according to directions. Meanwhile make ¼-inch cut with scissors in round backs of shrimps. Remove vein. Wash lobster-shrimp in colander. Do not remove shells. Turn them onto paper toweling to drain. Place 6 tablespoons butter in skillet. Sauté lobster-shrimp for one minute over high heat, turning them once. Pour one tablespoon brandy over the mixture in the skillet. Light match and hold close to shrimp until brandy flames. Continue to cook shrimp over low flame while you wash and chop shallots and parsley. Add shallots, parsley, thyme, 2 tablespoons tomato sauce, bay leaf, and one cup wine to skillet. Boil over high flame for 2 minutes. Stir in cream. Arrange rice and shrimp on serving dish. Pour sauce over rice. Serve hot.

GARNISH (*Optional*)
Tuck pieces of fresh parsley in among the lobster-shrimp. Peel and chop one black truffle and cook it in a little white wine for one minute. Drain truffle and sprinkle over lobster-shrimp and rice in serving bowl.

WINE
Pouilly-Fuissé, slightly chilled

SUKIYAKI

If you are tired of Chinese food there's another area of Oriental cooking you can explore. Japanese Sukiyaki has the excitement of the East about it, but in a different, more delicate way. Picture firm yet tender vegetables and succulent, thin beef slices, gently cooked in sweet salt beef broth and served on small opaque mountains of pearl-white rice. Fabulous!

INGREDIENTS

1 cup minute rice
½ pound thin sliced rare roast beef, available at any delicatessen
4 large mushrooms
3 five-inch pieces celery
¼ pound fresh spinach
4 scallions
1 medium size onion
3 tablespoons salad oil
½ 10½-ounce can consommé
2 tablespoons sugar
4 tablespoons soy sauce

ASSEMBLE

1 saucepan
1 iron skillet or other heavy skillet
paper towels
1 spoon
1 colander
1 set measuring spoons
1 paring knife
1 can opener
1 measuring cup

DIRECTIONS

Cook rice according to instructions on package. Put skillet on medium flame. Meanwhile peel onion and mushrooms. Slice. Add salad oil, onion, mushrooms, and roast beef to skillet. In colander wash spinach, scallions, and celery. Turn onto paper towels to drain. Quickly slice spinach into one-inch pieces. Slice celery and scallions into thin slices. Add to skillet. Add soy sauce, sugar, and consommé to skillet. Stir. Cook for 2 minutes. Stir again. Serve hot over the rice. (The Japanese serve each guest with a small bowl containing one raw, beaten egg into which each forkful may be dipped prior to eating. Tastes better than it sounds. Try it.)

LOBSTER PERNOD OR ABSINTHE GOURMET

If you would combine the exotic flavors of lobster, chervil, white wine, and Pernod (or absinthe) in one steaming caldron you would expect people to sit up and take notice. In this recipe you do, and they do!

INGREDIENTS

3 small lobsters, cooked. Available at your fish store. Ask to have them cut, shell and all, into 2-inch slices
1 cup white wine
3 tablespoons butter
1 tablespoon flour
¼ teaspoon salt
⅛ teaspoon white pepper
¼ cup Pernod (or absinthe)
1 tablespoon dried tarragon
1½ tablespoons dried chervil

ASSEMBLE

1 kettle
1 saucepan
1 set measuring spoons
1 measuring cup
1 butcher knife
1 nut cracker (pincher type)
1 spoon
1 serving dish
1 serving ladle

DIRECTIONS

Discard heads of lobsters, crack claws with nut cracker. Place pieces of lobster in kettle. Cover with one cup of white wine. Measure one tablespoon flour, 2 tablespoons butter, ¼ teaspoon salt, and ⅛ teaspoon pepper into saucepan. Melt butter. Stir until slightly thickened. Add one tablespoon tarragon and 1½ tablespoons chervil. Add one tablespoon butter to lobster meat. When hot add ¼ cup Pernod or absinthe. Set aflame. When flame is out add butter sauce. Bring to a boil, stirring constantly. Serve hot.

WINE
Pouilly-Fuissé, slightly chilled

BOEUF AU VIN BLANC

A lovely blending of beef and butter, shallots and white wine. Not overstated, not understated: just perfectly Parisienne.

INGREDIENTS

1 pound sliced rare roast beef, available at any delicatessen
3 tablespoons butter
2 shallots
1 small onion
3 tablespoons chopped parsley
5 tablespoons consommé
⅓ cup white wine
¼ teaspoon salt
⅛ teaspoon coarse black pepper
1 clove garlic

ASSEMBLE

1 medium size skillet
1 measuring cup
1 set measuring spoons
1 paring knife
1 can opener
1 garlic press
1 serving dish

DIRECTIONS

Wash, peel, and chop shallots and onion. Place onion, shallots, salt and pepper, butter, and meat in skillet. Cook for 2 minutes over high heat. Meanwhile measure wine, consommé. Add to skillet. Mash garlic in garlic press and add juice and pulp to skillet. Chop parsley. Add to skillet. Cook over high heat until sauce barely covers meat. Serve hot.

GARNISH

Finely chop two sprigs parsley. Sprinkle over beef. Serve immediately.

WINE

Pomerol, Bordeaux Heavy

KIDNEYS FLAMBÉ

Rich and delicious in a way only kidneys can be. Top them with bacon, shallots, mushrooms, and truffles (not to mention brandy and cream), and you won't believe what a marvelous cook you are.

INGREDIENTS
3 veal kidneys
3 strips bacon
2 scallions
2 small shallots
¼ teaspoon salt
1 large pinch of coarse black pepper
6 mushrooms
2 tablespoons butter
2 black truffles
2 tablespoons brandy
5 tablespoons heavy cream

ASSEMBLE
1 chafing dish
Sterno
1 paring knife
1 set measuring spoons
1 stirring spoon
1 serving plate

DIRECTIONS
Place bacon in blazer pan of chafing dish. Cook over low flame. Cut kidneys into thin slices, avoiding fat and membrane. Wash, peel, and thinly slice scallions, shallots, mushrooms, and truffles. Sauté kidneys in the bacon fat for one minute over high flame. Add scallions, shallots, mushrooms, butter, truffles, salt, and pepper to skillet. Cook over medium heat for 2 minutes. Add heavy cream to mixture in skillet. Stir. Pour brandy over kidneys. When warm set aflame. Serve hot.

GARNISH (*Optional*)

Along side of serving dish place one small, spiced apple. Place one leaf of watercress near stem of apple. Tuck small sprigs of watercress 2 inches apart around side of dish. Serve immediately.

WINE

Bordeaux Graves

SPAGHETTI WITH WHITE CLAM SAUCE

Breathes there the fine Italian restaurant that doesn't brag about its linguine? No, it's true they do, and rightly. Now you can too! Cook this for spaghetti with white clam sauce that's as good as any, anywhere.

INGREDIENTS

- 1 ½-pound box spaghetti or linguine
- 2 quarts boiling water
- 1 4-ounce can minced clams, or 1 dozen fresh clams
- 3 tablespoons olive oil
- ¼ pound butter
- 2 cloves crushed garlic
- 2 tablespoons orégano
- 1 tablespoon parsley flakes
- ¼ teaspoon salt
- ¼ teaspoon Tabasco sauce
- ⅛ teaspoon coarsely ground black pepper

ASSEMBLE

- 1 kettle or large pot
- 1 set measuring spoons
- 1 can opener
- 1 garlic press
- 1 medium size skillet
- 1 colander

DIRECTIONS

Place skillet over medium heat. Add 3 tablespoons olive oil, ¼ pound butter, one can minced clams (spoon clams and liquid into pan so as not to disturb sand which may be in the bottom of can), one tablespoon parsley flakes, ¼ teaspoon salt, and ¼ teaspoon Tabasco sauce. Peel and crush garlic into skillet. Cook until mixture begins to bubble. Meantime cook spaghetti al dente in boiling water according to directions on package, and drain. Place spaghetti in large serving dish and pour sauce over it. Sprinkle with 2 tablespoons orégano and ⅛ teaspoon black pepper. Toss spaghetti and sauce together before guests. Serve immediately.

WINE

Orvieto Secco, Italian Dry, slightly chilled

Salads

The perfect meal's perfect wife

Nothing is more important to the meal than the salad. Designed to cool the tongue and render it neutral and ready fully to appreciate the next course, the salad has become much more than that. It sets off the meal the way the perfect wife should set off her husband. If he is witty and full of ginger she should be calm and cool. If he is quiet and elegant she should contrast by sparkling with *joie de vivre*. If he is foreign and exotic she should perhaps contrast subtly or echo his continental charm but in a different way. That is not to say she should not have a winning and purposeful personality of her own: she should. So it is with a salad.

If the meal is hot and spicy the salad should be cool and green. If the meal is subtle and rather bland in its variations of flavor, the salad should be crunchy and tart. If the meal is a foreign or unusual one, the salad should complement the other courscs, but not fight for attention, or if you prefer, be an extension of the exotic flavors of the meal but with a different texture. Still, the salad should have character and subtleties within its own flavor structure, sometimes cooling the taste buds to prepare them for the next treat, sometimes zestful and seeming to say, "Wake Up! Something good is coming."

At all times the salad should be picked carefully. In its color, texture, and flavor, whether served before, after, or during the main course, a salad should always complement, beautifully, the meal it accompanies.

ONION SALAD

At last onions get the special treatment they deserve: a salad of their very own! Two varieties of sweet onions combine with an anchovy dressing to make a salad treat that adds ZOW to the blandest meal. If you like onions you'll love this.

INGREDIENTS

1 small red onion
1 small sweet Bermuda onion
16 pitted black olives
2 tablespoons wine vinegar
¼ cup olive oil
2 teaspoons anchovy paste
freshly ground black pepper to
    taste

ASSEMBLE

1 butcher knife
1 can opener
1 strainer
1 measuring cup
1 set measuring spoons
1 tablespoon
1 small mixing bowl
1 salad bowl

DIRECTIONS

Peel and cut onions into thin slices. Arrange neatly in salad bowl. Place bowl in refrigerator. Place 2 tablespoons vinegar, ¼ cup olive oil, and 2 teaspoons anchovy paste in mixing bowl. Beat vigorously. Open can of black olives and drain in strainer. Remove salad bowl from refrigerator, arrange 16 olives on top of onion slices. Stir dressing and pour over salad. Sprinkle with pepper. Serve cold.

LOBSTER SALAD*

This lobster salad is fit for a king. However, if you aren't expecting any kings, try it out on your favorite guests and prepare to be hailed as a Queen among cooks. Lobster, chicken, shrimp, turkey, and ham combine to make this the perfect main course salad for a luncheon or a late night snack. Try it also as a stuffing for tomatoes to serve with a cold meal. Delicious!

INGREDIENTS

2 cooked lobsters. Ask to have them split and the claws cracked.
¼ pound boiled sliced ham
¼ pound sliced turkey, available in any delicatessen
10 large cooked shrimp, available in your fish store
2 tablespoons capers, drained
10 stuffed green olives
3 heaping tablespoons mayonnaise
½ teaspoon salt
1 tablespoon tarragon vinegar
1 tablespoon olive oil
1 level teaspoon mustard, mild yellow
tomalley of lobster, if available
4 leaves of lettuce or escarole

ASSEMBLE

1 large mixing bowl
1 set measuring spoons
1 measuring cup
1 spoon
2 forks
1 paring knife
paper toweling
2 serving plates

DIRECTIONS

Remove meat from tail section of lobster without breaking shell. Cut into ½-inch slices. Cut 6 shrimps in pieces. Reserve 4 whole shrimps for trim. Place 3 heaping tablespoons mayonnaise, ½ teaspoon salt, one tablespoon vinegar, one tablespoon olive oil, one level teaspoon mustard, tomalley of lobster, and 10 whole olives in the mixing bowl. Stir. Cut ham and turkey in ½-inch strips. Add strips of ham and turkey, the chopped shrimps and lobster, and capers to mayonnaise mixture. Toss, using the two forks.

GARNISH

Wash lettuce and drain on paper toweling. Arrange lettuce leaves on salad plates. Place 1 split lobster on each plate. Mount the salad in the center of each lobster shell. Garnish with whole shrimps. Serve cold.

ADDITIONAL GARNISH (*Optional*)

Cook 3 black truffles in a little white wine for 3 minutes. Remove from liquid, and chop one of the truffles. Put a tablespoon of mayonnaise in the center of lobster salad and top with one whole truffle. Sprinkle the chopped truffle around the sides of the salad.

* May be prepared several hours in advance of serving. Refrigerate.

CUCUMBER SALAD DAMASCUS*

Does the meal you plan cry for something cool and unusually delicious? Then this is the salad at the end of the rainbow for you. Cucumber Salad Damascus has all the requirements necessary to go with the spicy meal. It is cool in texture, flavor, color, and temperature. In other words it's perfect. Better try it!

INGREDIENTS

1½ Cucumbers
¼ cup yoghurt
½ clove garlic
2 tablespoons chopped chives
1 tablespoon dried mint
salt and pepper to taste

ASSEMBLE

1 paring knife
1 measuring cup
1 set measuring spoons
1 spoon
1 garlic press
1 mixing bowl
1 tablespoon
1 salad bowl
salad fork and spoon

DIRECTIONS

Peel cucumbers and slice in thin slices. Place slices in mixing bowl. Measure ¼ cup yoghurt and leave in measuring cup. Peel ½ clove garlic and crush well in garlic press. Stir garlic and yoghurt together. Sprinkle salt and pepper on cucumbers. Toss cucumbers and yoghurt mixture together. Place cucumbers in salad bowl and sprinkle with 2 tablespoons chopped chives and one tablespoon dried mint. Serve cold.

NOTE

To serve 3 add ½ cucumber. To serve 4 double entire recipe.

* May be prepared an hour in advance of serving. Refrigerate until needed.

CAULIFLOWER SALAD*

An unexpected combination of ingredients makes this a salad of unusually subtle flavor. Cooked cauliflower, fried green pepper, sliced beets, French dressing, and a little tarragon seem magically to melt together to create a perfectly delicious salad. Serve at room temperature to enhance its mellow flavor.

INGREDIENTS

1 10-ounce package frozen cauliflower
1 green pepper
1 8-ounce can sliced beets
1 tablespoon butter
5 tablespoons French dressing
¼ teaspoon tarragon

ASSEMBLE

1 saucepan
1 skillet
1 paring knife
1 set measuring spoons
1 serving bowl
salad fork and spoon
salad plates

DIRECTIONS

Cook cauliflower according to directions on package. Meanwhile remove seeds from green pepper. Wash. Cut in one-inch slices. Sauté in one tablespoon butter for one minute. Open can of sliced beets. Drain. Arrange in salad bowl. Drain cauliflower. Arrange on beet slices. Add green pepper slices. Arrange nicely. Dribble 5 tablespoons French dressing over contents of salad bowl. Sprinkle with tarragon. Serve at room temperature.

*May be prepared several hours before serving time. Keep at room temperature.

FRUIT AND CUCUMBER SALAD

Looking for a salad everyone will like? Stop here! This combination of fresh fruit, cucumber, and French dressing is certain to please. As a matter of fact it's so good you can serve it for a main course at luncheon. Just decorate a plate with whole leaves of romaine lettuce, top with this salad, and decorate with halves of peaches, pears, and cherries. Then prepare to sit back and take bows. You're sure to get them.

INGREDIENTS

2 fresh peaches
4 halves canned pears
1 small or ½ large cucumber
20 Bing cherries
¼ cup French dressing

ASSEMBLE

1 paring knife
1 large salad bowl
1 measuring cup
salad fork and spoon

DIRECTIONS

Peel and slice thinly peaches and cucumber. Slice pears. Place in salad bowl. Cut 20 cherries in half, remove pits, and add cherry meats to salad bowl. Add ¼ cup French dressing. Toss. Serve immediately.

GARNISH (*Optional*)

Decorate center of salad by making a flower of cherry halves. Cut a small piece of peach and insert 2 whole cloves. Use as center of cherry flower. Cut a "stem" of cucumber peel and put at one side of the cherry flower. Place a whole mint leaf on either side of the cucumber peel "stem." Serve immediately.

CAESAR SALAD

Truly the Caesar among salads! If you have never fixed this don't wait another day for here is a recipe that is not only easy to prepare but completely delectable. Don't let the fame of this salad frighten you away. This recipe works every time.

INGREDIENTS

½ head romaine lettuce
3 tablespoons olive oil
¼ cup olive oil
2 cloves garlic
1 egg yolk
1 cup packaged croutons or 2
  slices day-old bread
¼ cup grated Parmesan cheese
1 teaspoon salt
1 tablespoon lemon juice
8 anchovy fillets (flat)
⅛ teaspoon pepper, coarsely
  ground

ASSEMBLE

1 small skillet
1 measuring cup
1 set measuring spoons
1 spoon
1 paring knife
1 garlic press
paper toweling
1 salad bowl
salad fork and spoon

DIRECTIONS

Fry one cup croutons in 3 tablespoons olive oil for one minute. Stir often. Wash ½ head of romaine lettuce. Drain on paper toweling. Peel garlic cloves. Crush in garlic press and place in salad bowl with one teaspoon salt. Mash garlic and salt together with back of spoon. Add one egg yolk. Mix. Add ¼ cup olive oil, one tablespoon lemon juice, and ⅛ teaspoon pepper. Mix. Break lettuce into 2-inch pieces and toss with dressing in salad bowl. Drain 8 anchovy fillets on paper toweling. Cut into fourths. Sprinkle ¼ cup grated Parmesan cheese, anchovies and croutons over salad. Serve immediately.

LEBANESE SALAD

Here is a salad that has everything: the "salady" flavor of tomato and romaine lettuce, the zest of scallions and mint, and the crunchiness of wheat germ. Top it all off with olive oil and vinegar and get ready to be surprised —pleasantly!

INGREDIENTS

1 large tomato
½ head romaine lettuce
2 scallions
2 tablespoons wheat germ
20 fresh mint leaves; 1 tablespoon
    dried mint may be substituted
    if necessary
3 tablespoons olive oil
3 tablespoons vinegar (white
    wine is best)
⅛ teaspoon salt
pepper to taste

ASSEMBLE

1 paring knife
1 salad bowl
1 set measuring spoons
paper toweling
salad fork and spoon
salad plates

DIRECTIONS

Wash ½ head romaine lettuce. Drain on paper toweling. Wash 2 scallions, one tomato, and 20 mint leaves. Break lettuce into one-inch pieces. Arrange in salad bowl. Cut roots from scallions. Chop scallions, tomato, and mint leaves. Arrange on lettuce in salad bowl. Sprinkle 3 tablespoons olive oil and 3 tablespoons vinegar over salad. Sprinkle with ⅛ teaspoon salt, 2 tablespoons wheat germ, and pepper to taste. Serve cold.

ITALIAN WHITE BEAN AND ANCHOVY SALAD*

A white bean salad similar to and yet different from the French one. It starts the same way, with the smooth richness of white beans and olive oil and then the dash and excitement of Italian cooking takes over to create a "sit-up-and-take-notice" salad spiked with anchovies and black olives. It's really good!

INGREDIENTS

1½ cups white beans, measured after rinsing heavy juice from beans in colander
10 black olives, pitted
4 anchovy fillets, flat
1 clove garlic
2 sprigs parsley
½ teaspoon basil leaf (dried)
¼ cup olive oil
1 tablespoon lemon juice (bottled)
1 tablespoon capers

ASSEMBLE

1 large mixing bowl
1 small mixing bowl
1 can opener
1 garlic press
1 paring knife
1 set measuring spoons
1 colander
1 measuring cup
paper toweling
1 salad bowl
salad fork and spoon

DIRECTIONS

Open can of white beans. Place in colander. Rinse very quickly with water. Drain. Measure 1½ cups of white beans. Slice 10 olives into circles and add to beans. Open can of anchovies. Remove 4. Drain on paper toweling. Cut anchovies into quarters. Add to large mixing bowl along with beans, olives and one tablespoon capers. Measure ¼ cup olive oil. Pour into small mixing bowl. Peel clove of garlic. Force through garlic press into olive oil. Scrape garlic press and add pulp to small bowl. Add one tablespoon lemon juice and stir well. Pour over bean salad mixture and toss lightly. Place bean salad in salad bowl.

GARNISH

Wash and chop 2 sprigs of parsley. Sprinkle salad with chopped parsley and ½ teaspoon dried basil leaves. Serve at room temperature.

* May be prepared 24 hours in advance. Refrigerate. Allow to come to room temperature before serving.

Start with a head of lettuce and carry on from there. The following are recipes that can turn simple, fresh greens into salads par excellence with a mere flip of the wrist.

CREAMY BLUE CHEESE SALAD DRESSING

An extra special blue cheese dressing that is smooth and unusually flavored with chervil, tarragon, and nutmeg. Subtle, but pungent enough to give character to almost any combination of greens.

INGREDIENTS	ASSEMBLE
5 tablespoons blue cheese	1 mixing bowl
½ cup heavy cream	1 set measuring spoons
3 tablespoons lemon juice	1 measuring cup
½ teaspoon chervil	1 spoon
1 teaspoon tarragon	
¼ teaspoon salt	
⅛ teaspoon coarse black pepper	
1 generous pinch nutmeg	
1 pinch garlic powder	

DIRECTIONS

Mix 5 tablespoons blue cheese and ½ cup heavy cream until smooth. Add the remaining ingredients and mix thoroughly. Serve cold.

GREEN GODDESS SALAD DRESSING*

Delicate green and serene is this blender-smooth dressing for salads. Make it in an instant and serve it on Bibb lettuce for a salad amiable enough to accompany any meal. Good with seafood, too.

INGREDIENTS

½ cup mayonnaise
¼ cup sour cream
1 tablespoon tarragon vinegar
1 tablespoon lemon juice
1 tablespoon frozen chopped onion
2 anchovy fillets
1 tablespoon chopped scallion tops
2 tablespoons dried parsley flakes
1 peeled clove garlic
⅛ teaspoon black pepper

ASSEMBLE

1 measuring cup
1 set measuring spoons
1 blender
1 paring knife
1 spoon or rubber spatula

DIRECTIONS

Place all ingredients in electric blender container. Cover and blend at high speed for about 20 seconds. Stop blender and scrape down sides of container with spoon or spatula. Blend for 10 seconds more. Serve cold.

* May be prepared 24 hours in advance of serving. Refrigerate until needed.

ANTIPASTO SALAD DRESSING*

Here's a salad treat with the Zip! of vegetables right in the dressing. All you need is crisp lettuce to create a salad that's not only good to eat but colorful as well.

INGREDIENTS

½ cup olive oil
5 tablespoons red wine vinegar
2 tablespoons chopped onion
1 tablespoon chopped green pepper
1 tablespoon pitted and chopped
   black olives
1 tablespoon chopped pimento
2 slices salami
2 cloves crushed garlic
⅛ teaspoon salt

ASSEMBLE

1 small mixing bowl
1 set measuring spoons
1 measuring cup
1 garlic press
1 paring knife

DIRECTIONS

Chop finely 2 tablespoons onion, one tablespoon green pepper, one tablespoon pimento, and one tablespoon black olives. Slice salami into very fine strips about one inch long. Place all chopped vegetables in mixing bowl with ½ cup olive oil, 5 tablespoons red wine vinegar, and ⅛ teaspoon salt. Crush 2 garlic cloves into mixing bowl. Add salami and stir vigorously. Serve cold.

* May be prepared 24 hours in advance of serving. Refrigerate until needed.

Vegetables
Silent partners of the meal

Hors d'oeuvres are beautiful promises, soups are liquid gold, salads are pace-changers, entrées are promises come true. Is there nothing in a meal that is unimportant? No, but there are some things that are less important than others, and vegetables fall into that category.

Vegetables are of less importance than any other single element in a meal, but only if they are chosen with care. The more carefully they are chosen, the less important they become. Then why pick them carefully? Simply because vegetables are performing their function perfectly if they blend smoothly and unobtrusively with the rest of the meal. Of course they should be perfectly prepared, colorful, and wonderfully tasty, but equally important, they should be minor planets totally eclipsed by their entrée.

The best thing I can think of to determine if the vegetables you have chosen are right for the meal they are to accompany is to taste the main course and the vegetables together to see if they blend. They can differ but they must blend well. After a little practice you will be able to do your "tasting" mentally and avoid a lot of trouble. Just "think" the tastes of your entrée and vegetables, one after the other, and if one seems to jar your "mental" taste buds it is likely something should be changed. To see if your mental tester is operating properly, "think" two foods that do not seem to go well together, such as shrimp and garlic butter with sugar and heavy cream. Ugh. Now "think" two foods that go marvelously together such as prosciutto and melon. Yum. Every time you prepare a meal try this test before you actually taste anything. Before long you'll be able to pick up a cookbook and "taste" your way into seventh heaven.

After you have taste-tested the vegetables you have chosen to accompany your dinner, test them for eye appeal. Visualize them on the dishes from which they are to be eaten. White against white? Fine if dressed up with pieces of black truffle, a touch of paprika, a border of parsley. But if everything in the meal is light or white, shouldn't you use a vegetable with a similar taste but a different color?

And what about texture? Before you choose a creamed vegetable, go over your menu and be sure you haven't inadvertently chosen a creamy hors d'oeuvre, a cream soup, a salad with a creamy dressing, an entrée in a rich, creamy sauce and . . . I'm sure you haven't, but the tastes do go well together and it is easy to get so excited over an individual dish that you don't realize until too late that the foods you've chosen are too similar.

Summing up then, carefully choose the vegetables to round out the meal but to be completely subordinate to the entrée. They should be secondary but never drab, silently impressive, always backing the main course with a show of quiet strength.

GREEN ONIONS WITH LEMON-CLAM SAUCE

Tender, cooked green onions with a lovely, lemony, clam sauce. Perfect with almost any meal.

INGREDIENTS

12 young green onions or scallions, about the thickness of a pencil
1 cup hot water
6 tablespoons butter
1 tablespoon lemon juice
4 tablespoons minced clams

ASSEMBLE

1 cooking pan with 8-inch bottom
1 skillet
1 set measuring spoons
1 tablespoon
paper towels
2 individual serving plates

DIRECTIONS

Place hot water and washed, trimmed scallions in cooking pan. Cook over high flame for 4 minutes. Meanwhile melt butter in skillet. Add lemon juice and minced clams. Heat. Drain scallions and place on paper towels. Place hot scallions, 6 each, on the two plates. Reheat clam sauce if not hot. Divide sauce evenly on the two mounds of scallions. Serve hot.

NOTE

When trimming scallions leave 4 inches of green top.

GARLIC CHERRY
TOMATOES

*Round, red bits of goodness—cherry tomatoes all warm
and buttery and sprinkled with garlic. Marvelous as a
vegetable, attractive as a garnish and capable of func-
tioning as both at once!*

INGREDIENTS

1 pint box cherry tomatoes
¼ pound butter
1 teaspoon garlic powder
salt and coarse black pepper if
    desired

ASSEMBLE

1 skillet
1 set measuring spoons
1 tablespoon
1 serving dish

DIRECTIONS

Place skillet over low heat. Add butter. Melt. Add garlic powder
to butter. Heat but do not brown. Add tomatoes. Heat for 4
minutes over very low flame. Sprinkle with salt and pepper to
taste. Serve immediately.

GARNISH (*Optional*)

Place tomatoes on a bed of watercress. Tuck sprigs of watercress among tomatoes. Serve hot.

FLUFFY CORN FRITTERS

Light-as-a-feather corn fritters, fantastic when topped with maple syrup or simply delicious when served on their own.

INGREDIENTS

4 large ears fresh corn
4 egg whites
salt
¼ cup vegetable oil

ASSEMBLE

1 skillet
1 grater
1 table knife
1 rotary beater
2 mixing bowls
1 measuring cup

DIRECTIONS

Grate as much corn as is possible by rubbing the ears of corn against the grater. Scrape the cob with a table knife to remove any remaining juice. In another bowl beat the egg whites until stiff. Put the salad oil in the skillet and heat to moderate-high. Gently fold the beaten egg whites into the grated corn. Do not stir or mix too roughly. Spoon the corn and egg white mixture a tablespoonful at a time into the hot oil. Fry until golden and then turn gently and fry until done. Sprinkle with salt. Serve immediately while very hot.

CARROTS AND WHITE GRAPES

A vegetable dish that is colorful yet tasty in a dignified, understated way. You'll be surprised how well grapes behave as a vegetable.

INGREDIENTS

1 13½-ounce can small whole Belgian carrots
30 seedless white grapes
4 tablespoons Cointreau (optional)
4 tablespoons butter

ASSEMBLE

1 skillet
1 set measuring spoons
paper toweling
1 tablespoon
1 serving bowl

DIRECTIONS

Open can of carrots. Drain on paper towels. Wash grapes. Place on paper towels to dry. Place skillet over medium flame. Add butter. When butter has melted add Cointreau. Stir. Add grapes and carrots and cook over low flame for 4 minutes. Stir frequently. Serve hot.

NOTE

To serve 3 add 20 grapes. To serve 4, double recipe.

GARNISH

Tuck pairs of fresh mint leaves here and there among grapes and carrots. Serve hot.

FRIED GREEN PEPPERS*

Green peppers in a slightly different role: fried and served as a vegetable on their own, or very nearly so. Onions do their bit and so does French dressing, but the green peppers are really the star of the show.

INGREDIENTS

3 green peppers
2 small onions
1 tablespoon olive oil
1 tablespoon butter
2 tablespoons French dressing
pinch dry mustard

ASSEMBLE

1 skillet
1 paring knife
1 set measuring spoons
paper toweling
1 serving dish

DIRECTIONS

Remove pulp and seeds from 3 green peppers. Wash. Dry with paper toweling. Peel, wash, and slice 2 onions into rings. Place one tablespoon olive oil and one tablespoon butter in skillet. Slice green peppers into one-inch strips. Add green pepper strips and onion slices to skillet. Fry over medium flame until onions just begin to brown. Remove from heat and add 2 tablespoons French dressing and one pinch dry mustard. Stir until mixed. Serve immediately.

* May be prepared an hour in advance of serving. Fry peppers and onions for 2 minutes only and remove from flame. Five minutes before serving time continue frying for 3 or 4 minutes more. Add French dressing and serve hot.

VEGETABLES IN CREAM

If you're tired of the same old mixed vegetables, keep this recipe in mind. The real surprise is the lettuce, a vegetable often cooked in France but seldom in America. You won't be sorry if you try it.

INGREDIENTS

8 scallions
½ 10-ounce package frozen peas
   and carrots
½ head lettuce
2 tablespoons water
¼ teaspoon sugar
4 tablespoons butter
4 tablespoons heavy cream

ASSEMBLE

1 saucepan
1 set measuring spoons
1 skillet with cover
1 colander
1 spoon
1 paring knife
paper toweling
1 serving dish

DIRECTIONS

Cook peas and carrots according to directions on package. Meanwhile, wash ½ head of lettuce and drain on paper toweling. Wash scallions and cut off roots. Cut 4 scallions into pieces ½ inch long, including several inches of the green end. Slice lettuce into strips ½ inch wide and 3 inches long. Melt 4 tablespoons butter in skillet. Add ¼ teaspoon sugar, lettuce, chopped scallions plus 4 whole scallions, and two tablespoons water. Cover and steam cook over medium heat for 3 minutes. If skillet should cook dry add 2 more tablespoons water. Add 4 tablespoons heavy cream. Cook without boiling for one minute. Drain peas and carrots. Mound peas, carrots, and chopped scallions in center of serving dish. Place cooked lettuce on one side of serving dish and cooked whole scallions on the other side. Serve hot.

NOTE

To serve 3 use entire package of peas and carrots and one additional scallion. To serve 4 double entire recipe.

GARNISH (*Optional*)

Criss-cross scallions with strips of pimento. Sprinkle peas, carrots, and chopped scallions with one tablespoon hard-cooked egg yolk pushed through a sieve. Place one slice hard cooked egg on lettuce strips. Top with one caper. Serve hot.

CAULIFLOWER WITH ALMONDS

A marvelous combination of tastes. Crispy almonds and golden crumbs crowning snowy-white flowerlets of cauliflower and garlic to make it naughty but nice.

INGREDIENTS

1 10-ounce package frozen cauliflower
½ cup bread crumbs
¼ cup butter
¾ cup slivered almonds
1 clove garlic, minced
1 teaspoon salt

ASSEMBLE

1 saucepan
1 skillet
1 spoon
1 serving dish

DIRECTIONS

Cook cauliflower according to directions on package. Sauté butter, crumbs, almonds, and garlic in skillet until almonds and crumbs are golden in color. Pour over cauliflower. Serve hot.

GARNISH (*Optional*)

Tuck small pieces of parsley among the cauliflower flowerlets, sprinkle with paprika. Serve hot.

GREEN BEANS AND ONIONS AU BEURRE*

You'll have to taste it to believe just how much flavor can be released by using just the right tablespoon of just the right ingredient in just the right place.

INGREDIENTS	ASSEMBLE
½ 9-ounce package frozen green beans (cut green beans, Italian green beans, Frenched green beans all equally delicious prepared this way)	1 medium size saucepan
	1 medium size skillet
	1 set measuring spoons
	1 paring knife
	1 spoon
½ teaspoon salt	1 serving dish
4 tablespoons butter	
2 small onions	
1 tablespoon wine vinegar	

DIRECTIONS

Cook beans according to directions on package. Meanwhile melt butter in skillet. Peel the onions, slice into thin slices and add to skillet. Cook. Drain cooked beans. Add to skillet. Cook until both beans and onions begin to brown. Add vinegar, stir, and serve hot.

NOTE

To serve 3, double quantity of frozen string beans. To serve 4 double entire recipe.

* May be prepared in advance and reheated at serving time.

GREEN BEANS SERBIAN*

This is really something special! Drained green beans mixed with crumbs sautéed golden brown in butter, finely minced parsley stirred in, and the whole casserole topped with sour cream and baked. A hit every time!

INGREDIENTS

1 9-ounce package frozen green beans
salt according to directions on package
⅓ cup sweet butter
2 tablespoons bread crumbs
¼ cup minced parsley
½ teaspoon garlic powder
¾ cup sour cream
¼ teaspoon coarsely ground black pepper

ASSEMBLE

1 saucepan
1 skillet
1 measuring cup
1 colander
1 set measuring spoons
1 paring knife
1 tablespoon
1 flameproof dish or casserole

DIRECTIONS

Light oven. Set at 450°. Cook green beans in sauce pan according to directions on package. Meanwhile place skillet over medium high heat. Add butter. When melted add bread crumbs. Stir until lightly browned. Remove from flame. Thoroughly wash and dry parsley. Mince parsley with paring knife. Drain green beans in colander. Put green beans, parsley, breadcrumb mixture, garlic, and pepper in baking dish. Stir.* Spread sour cream over bean mixture. Bake for 2 minutes. Serve immediately.

GARNISH (*Optional*)

Cut lemon to form a cup topped with points. Scoop out lemon. Fill with a large dollop of sour cream. Place in center of sour-cream-covered beans. Arrange small strips of pimento and lemon rind and 4 pieces of green bean in a design radiating out from the lemon cup. Sprinkle a border of finely chopped parsley around the edge of the sour cream. Place a pinch of paprika at 2-inch intervals around sour cream, close to the parsley border. Bake 2 minutes, as above. Serve hot. Sprinkle chopped parsley around sour cream in lemon cup. Dot center of cup with pimento squares.

* May be prepared several hours in advance of serving. Bring recipe to this point. Heat beans in oven 10 minutes prior to serving.

NEW PEAS WITH MINT

Do you need an unobtrusive vegetable to round out the meal you have planned? This may be the very one you've been looking for. Tender new peas get together with butter, orégano, and just enough mint to keep them from being dull. A quiet spot with a lot of flavor.

INGREDIENTS

1 10-ounce package frozen new or baby peas
½ cup fresh mint leaves; 1½ tablespoons dried mint leaves may be substituted if necessary
¼ teaspoon salt
2 tablespoons butter
¼ teaspoon orégano

ASSEMBLE

1 saucepan
1 measuring cup
1 colander
1 paring knife
1 serving dish

DIRECTIONS

Cook peas according to directions on package. Break mint leaves from stems. Chop coarsely, until mint leaves measure ½ cup. Drain peas. Place 2 tablespoons butter in saucepan. Melt over medium heat. Add peas. Stir. Add chopped mint leaves and ¼ teaspoon orégano. Toss. Serve hot.

NOTE

Serves 2 or 3.

GARNISH

Reserve 2 tablespoons of the chopped mint and sprinkle with ⅛ teaspoon orégano over top of peas. Tuck whole mint leaves here and there among the peas. Serve hot.

ARTICHOKES WITH FOIE GRAS

This is a marvelous vegetable to serve with any meal that needs "a shot in the arm." Its rich, smooth combination of flavors seems to say, "This is a special meal for special people."

INGREDIENTS

4 artichoke bottoms (canned)
4 slices of foie gras
32 drops lemon juice
¼ teaspoon salt
2 tablespoons butter
1 tablespoon flour
1 cup heavy cream
7 tablespoons packaged grated
   Swiss or Cheddar cheese

ASSEMBLE

1 can opener
1 sharp knife
1 set measuring spoons
1 measuring cup
1 medium size skillet
1 spoon
1 flameproof serving dish

DIRECTIONS

Turn broiler flame on high. Sprinkle each artichoke base with 8 drops of lemon juice. Top each artichoke bottom with slice of foie gras. Melt butter in skillet. Add flour and salt. Stir until smooth. Pour in heavy cream and 4 tablespoons grated cheese. Stir until fairly thick. Place pâté-topped artichoke bottoms in flameproof dish. Pour sauce over artichokes and foie gras. Sprinkle with 3 tablespoons grated cheese. Place under broiler flame until top begins to turn golden.

Go withs

*"Little extras" that make
the difference*

Often in a really fine restaurant you will find "little extras" used to enhance the flavor or the appearance of the more important or substantial portions of the meal. Like a butterfly perched on a flower, the "go with" calls attention to the dish it accompanies without detracting in the least from its own beauty.

These eye- and palate-pleasing garnishes can make the difference between a really good meal that somehow fails to excite and a superb meal that is long remembered by the fortunate guests.

Serving Boeuf Au Vin? Marvelous! Your friends will love it, but as delicious as it is, it will never be as exciting looking as

a fancy shrimp curry. Oh no? Decorate the serving plate liber-
ally with anchovies in cherry tomatoes. Surround it completely
with sprigs of parsley and prepare to make an impression.

Treating your guests to Breast of Chicken in Rum Crumbs?
Top with Marrons in Apricot Halves and see a dish that's delicious but plain Jane in looks become a show stopper.

Use garnishes whenever you get the chance and never hesitate
to garnish the garnish.

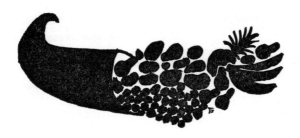

MARRONS AND APRICOTS

Here is a handsome garnish that has even more flavor than eye-appeal. The mellow goodness of marrons combined with honey-brushed apricots make a "go with" par excellence.

INGREDIENTS

4 marrons glacès, available bottled in syrup
2 fresh apricots
1 tablespoon honey
1 tablespoon butter

ASSEMBLE

1 paring knife
1 pastry brush
1 small baking dish

DIRECTIONS

Light broiler. Set on high flame. Wash and dry apricots. Cut in half and remove pits. Brush apricot halves with honey. Place in greased baking dish. Broil for one minute. Remove from broiler. Top each apricot half with one marron. Replace dish in broiler. Broil for one more minute. Serve hot or cold. Perfect garnish for any kind of game bird.

FRIED BANANAS

A "go with" more tempting to the palate than to the eye are these golden little rolls of fried banana. Serve hot with chicken, ham, curry, or any island meal for that extra embellishment that makes a meal something special.

INGREDIENTS

2 firm bananas
1 egg
¼ cup bread crumbs
3 tablespoons light rum
¼ cup cooking oil

ASSEMBLE

1 paring knife
1 small bowl
1 fork
2 plates
1 skillet
1 measuring cup
paper toweling

DIRECTIONS

Peel and slice bananas into one-inch pieces. Sprinkle with rum. Meanwhile beat egg in small bowl and place cooking oil in skillet. Place skillet over high heat. Dip banana pieces in egg and then roll in breadcrumbs. Drop into hot oil and fry until golden brown. Serve hot.

GRILLED CHEESE TOMATOES

These luscious cheese-topped grilled tomatoes provide an eye-filling, taste-thrilling garnish to more meals than you can shake a fork at. Particularly good with steak or any plain meat dish.

INGREDIENTS

2 tomatoes
3 shallots
4 tablespoons butter
3 tablespoons fine breadcrumbs
3 tablespoons grated Swiss cheese
1 tablespoon grated Parmesan cheese
⅛ teaspoon garlic powder
⅛ teaspoon salt

ASSEMBLE

1 shallow baking dish
1 set measuring spoons
1 paring knife
1 skillet
1 spoon

DIRECTIONS

Turn broiler on high flame. Wash tomatoes. Cut in half and shake out the seeds. Grease baking dish and place tomato halves on it. Dot tomatoes with butter. Place under broiler. Meanwhile, peel, wash, and chop shallots. Place 4 tablespoons butter in skillet. Add shallots and cook for a few seconds over medium heat. Add 3 tablespoons bread crumbs, one tablespoon grated Parmesan cheese, and ⅛ teaspoon each of salt and garlic powder. Stir. Remove baking dish from broiler. Divide the cheese-breadcrumb mixture evenly among the four tomato halves. Top each with one tablespoon grated Swiss cheese. Replace under broiler for one minute. Serve very hot.

ANCHOVIES IN CHERRY TOMATOES*

A tiny but toothsome garnish that's equally tasty served hot or cold. Arrange them like little roses with watercress for leaves and they'll dress up any dish.

INGREDIENTS

10 cherry tomatoes
5 teaspoons fine bread crumbs
10 rolled anchovy fillets
2 teaspoons anchovy oil
¼ teaspoon garlic powder
1 level teaspoon drained capers

ASSEMBLE

1 small bowl
1 paring knife
1 very small spoon
1 set measuring spoons

DIRECTIONS

Slice ¼ inch off the top of each cherry tomato. With small spoon scoop out tomato pulp. In small bowl combine bread crumbs, garlic powder, anchovy oil, and drained capers. Stir until well mixed. Fill each cherry tomato half full of bread crumb mixture. Top with rolled anchovy fillet. Anchovy should protrude from top of tomato. Use as garnish for any salad, steak, or Tartar Steak. Serve hot or cold.

* These can be prepared up to 2 hours in advance of serving. To heat place under broiler for a minute or two.

FANCY CHEESE CROUTONS FOR SOUP

Just the thing to turn any hot soup into a gourmet treat is this large, garlic flavored, cheese topped, garnished crouton. Soup lovers take note.

INGREDIENTS

2 slices French bread ½ inch thick; bread slices should not be too large
⅛ teaspoon garlic powder
2 tablespoons butter
2 tablespoons grated Swiss cheese
2 rolled anchovies
10 small strips pimento
12 capers

ASSEMBLE

1 bread knife
1 set measuring spoons
1 medium size skillet
paper toweling

DIRECTIONS

Turn broiler on high flame. Drain 10 small pimento strips and 2 anchovies on paper toweling. Place 2 tablespoons butter and ⅛ teaspoon garlic powder in skillet. Sauté the 2 slices of French bread in the butter until beginning to brown. Remove slices and place on paper toweling. Sprinkle each slice thickly with grated Swiss cheese. Place a rolled anchovy fillet in the center of each slice of cheese-topped bread. Arrange the pimento strips around the anchovy fillet, radiating outward. Place 3 capers on either side of the pimento strips. Place under broiler until cheese begins to brown.

PETITE PEAS IN ARTICHOKE BOTTOMS

Here's a garnish that doubles as a vegetable: a very superior combination of vegetables in a very sophisticated sauce. This special recipe is bound to become a specialty of yours.

INGREDIENTS

4 artichoke bottoms, canned, 12-ounce can
½ can petite peas
¼ cup red wine
1 shallot
1 small bay leaf
1 pinch marjoram
1 pinch of thyme
1 pinch of black pepper
⅓ teaspoon salt
¼ cup canned consommé (undiluted)
3 level tablespoons butter
10 drops lemon juice
10 drops vinegar (white wine)
1 teaspoon parsley flakes

ASSEMBLE

1 small saucepan
1 can opener
1 paring knife
1 measuring cup
1 set measuring spoons
1 tablespoon
1 small skillet
1 small strainer
1 sauce boat

DIRECTIONS

Set peas to heat in small saucepan. Drain 4 artichoke bottoms and place in skillet. Wash and chop shallot. Place shallot, one tablespoon butter, and vinegar in skillet. Heat for one minute. Remove artichokes. Place in serving dish. Add wine, bay leaf, marjoram, thyme, parsley flakes, pepper, and salt to skillet. Boil for one minute. Add consommé to sauce in skillet. Boil for 2

minutes. Strain sauce into cup. Return to skillet. Stir in lemon juice and butter. Drain peas. Add peas and artichoke bottoms to sauce for one minute. Remove artichoke bottoms from pan. Place on serving dish. Mound peas on artichoke bottoms. Serve remaining sauce separately. Serve hot.

GARNISH (*Optional*)
Place large slice cooked carrot on each mound of peas. Top carrot slice with one small slice black truffle, topped with a tiny amount sieved hard-cooked egg yolk, topped with one caper. Serve hot.

FLAMING SPICED PEACHES

If you love the effect of foods served flambé but think it's too much trouble to be worthwhile, here's a simple garnish that provides maximum taste with minimum trouble. Flame these peaches with brandy and serve with any fowl or game bird, or alone as a dessert.

INGREDIENTS

4 freestone peach halves or whole spiced peaches
¼ cup honey
¼ cup brandy
3 whole cloves for every peach half

ASSEMBLE

1 chafing dish
Sterno
1 can opener
1 measuring cup
1 ladle

DIRECTIONS

Drain juice from peaches. Decorate each peach half or spiced peach with 3 cloves. Arrange peaches, flat side down, in blazer pan of chafing dish. Heat for one minute over low flame. Add most of brandy to peaches. Pour the rest into the ladle. Heat by holding a match under the ladle. When brandy is warm light with a match. Pour the flaming brandy over the peaches and brandy in the chafing dish. When flame goes out stir in ¼ cup honey. Allow to bubble for a minute. Serve hot.

CURRIED PINEAPPLE SLICES

A marvelous "go with" for a wide variety of meals. You'll love it served with game, fowl, or any meal inspired by the islands. Also delicious with curry.

INGREDIENTS

4 slices canned pineapple
12 maraschino cherries
2 tablespoons butter
4 tablespoons pineapple liquid
2 tablespoons sugar
1 tablespoon rum
¼ teaspoon curry powder

ASSEMBLE

1 medium sized skillet
1 can opener
1 spoon
1 set measuring spoons

DIRECTIONS

Place 2 tablespoons butter in skillet. Melt over medium heat. Add 4 tablespoons pineapple liquid, 2 tablespoons sugar, one tablespoon rum, and ¼ teaspoon curry powder. Stir over high heat for one minute. Add 4 pineapple slices and cherries. Cook over high heat for 2 minutes. Serve hot or cold.

HAM CORNUCOPIAS

Roll up a few of these cornucopias the next time you're serving a cold salad or cold buffet. You'll find them tasty, handy, and decorative trim for nearly anything.

INGREDIENTS

4 large, thin slices of cold boiled ham, available delicatessen
2 tablespoons crab meat
1 3-ounce package cream cheese
½ cup finely chopped pistachio or walnut meats
1 tablespoon heavy cream
2 tablespoons finely chopped celery

ASSEMBLE

1 small mixing bowl
1 fork
1 teaspoon
1 paring knife

DIRECTIONS

Place package of cream cheese in mixing bowl along with one tablespoon heavy cream. Mix until creamy. Add 2 tablespoons crab meat, 2 tablespoons celery and ¼ cup nut meats, all finely chopped. Mix. Lay ham slice out flat. Spoon on 3 tablespoons full cream cheese nut mixture. Roll ham slice into cornucopia. Allow some of cheese mixture to protrude from the open end. Dip this end in the remaining chopped nuts. Repeat process with each ham slice. Serve cold.

GLAZED APPLE RINGS

Decorate roast pork, roast chicken, pork chops, or ham with these spicy, red glazed apple rings for a touch of color and a ton of taste. As a garnish at Christmas time color some green. Even Saint Nick will stay for dinner.

INGREDIENTS

3 medium size apples
½ teaspoon nutmeg
½ teaspoon cinnamon
¼ teaspoon ground cloves
3 tablespoons butter
¼ cup brown sugar
1 teaspoon plus 6 drops red food coloring
1 tablespoon water

ASSEMBLE

1 shallow baking dish
1 cup (for food coloring)
1 apple corer
1 paring knife
1 set measuring spoons
1 small bowl
1 measuring cup

DIRECTIONS

Set broiler on high flame. Peel and core apples. Slice into rings ½ inch thick. Mix one teaspoon red food coloring with one tablespoon water. Dip apple slices in food coloring, pat dry. Dot bottom of baking dish with butter. Place apple rings in baking dish. Mix sugar with 6 drops food coloring. Sprinkle apple slices with the sugar and spices and place under broiler until sugar becomes glazed. Serve hot.

Desserts

The sirens of the dinner

The most elegant yet the most flamboyant moment in a meal is often that course with the combined elements of innocence and excitement: the dessert.

With all the care and concern lavished on the rest of the meal, no matter how important or imposing the entrée, it is generally the dessert that is the siren of the dinner.

This final course not only holds its own among the other delectable elements of the meal, but generally steals hearts with outrageous lack of concern for the dignity of the main course.

But for all its scene stealing, the dessert must not be singled out for this reason alone. It is most important that the choice of dessert be arrived at systematically through the selection of first the main course, then the first course and soup, the vegetables and salad and finally a dessert that will do the most for not only itself but the rest of the meal.

Select a light syrupy or fruity dessert such as Pêches Flambées for a meal that tends to be slightly heavy. Decide upon a rich creamy trifle as a close for a moderately plain or meaty English meal.

Or flame up a chafing dish of that perfection, Crêpes Suzette, as an exciting climax to that meal of many minor climaxes, the French dinner.

A bewitching variety of desserts is available but all have one function: to culminate the meal and render it perfect.

CHAMPAGNE FRUIT COCKTAIL

A ladylike dessert? Perhaps, but one that may tend to mellow the lady considerably. On the other hand her companion may be too involved with dessert to notice. If he is, more's the pity. A terrible waste to serve to more than two.

INGREDIENTS

4 canned peach halves
10 large fresh strawberries
4 sugar cubes soaked with bitters
1 bottle iced champagne

ASSEMBLE

1 can opener
1 cork screw
2 champagne glasses
1 serving plate
1 serving spoon

DIRECTIONS

Open can of peaches. Drain 4 halves. Remove stems from strawberries. Arrange fruit on serving plate. Top each peach half with one cube of sugar soaked with bitters. Be careful not to dissolve sugar cubes with bitters. Just dampen them. Open champagne. At table, place one peach half with sugar cube and several strawberries in each champagne glass. Pour champagne over fruit. The fruit-champagne ratio depends on the consumer's addiction to either fruit or champagne.

PÊCHES FLAMBÉES

Fresh, ripe peaches, poached in syrup, set like a golden crown on a mound of macaroon crumbs, and finally, flamed with Cointreau. A perfect dessert. Not too heavy but rich enough to satisfy the most avid dessert eater.

INGREDIENTS

2 fully ripe peaches
¾ cup boiling water
¾ cup sugar
10 drops lemon juice
4 tablespoons Cointreau. Rum may be substituted.
8 tablespoons macaroon crumbs or 4 macaroons
1 cup boiling water

ASSEMBLE

1 pyrex bowl
1 paring knife
1 small saucepan
1 set measuring spoons
1 box matches
1 chafing dish (2 quart size)
1 serving spoon
2 serving plates

DIRECTIONS

Place peaches in pyrex bowl. Pour one cup boiling water over them. Lift out one peach, cut in half, and gently remove the pit. Gently pull off the skin with paring knife. Repeat process with remaining peach halves. Place ¾ cup boiling water and ¾ cup sugar in saucepan. Place over high flame. Add peach halves and 10 drops lemon juice to syrup in pan. Boil for 4 minutes. Meanwhile make 2 mounds of macaroon crumbs on each serving plate. Each mound should consist of 2 tablespoons macaroon crumbs. Turn off flame under the peaches. Place peaches and syrup in blazer pan of chafing dish. Arrange serving plates with macaroon crumbs on tray. When ready to serve carry chafing dish and serving plates to table. Heat peaches and syrup over medium flame. Pour Cointreau gently over peaches in syrup. Do not stir. Light Cointreau with a match. This will be easy after the Cointreau is heated slightly by the hot syrup. Place a peach half on each mound of crumbs. Spoon 6 table-spoons of Cointreau-syrup mixture over each peach half. Serve warm.

APPLE COINTREAU SUNDAE

If this sounds too easy to be good you have a pleasant surprise in store. Fresh, crispy apple slices combined with ice cream would be a treat even without the satiny smooth taste of the Cointreau, but with it . . . well, taste it and see!

INGREDIENTS

1 fresh apple
2 scoops vanilla ice cream
2 tablespoons Cointreau

ASSEMBLE

1 ice cream scoop
1 paring knife
silver dishes

DIRECTIONS

Peel the apple and cut into thin unbroken slices. Arrange neatly around edge of the dishes. Scoop out large scoop of ice cream and place in the middle of the apple slices. Add Cointreau. Serve immediately.

GARNISH

Place 2 slices of apple in center of ice cream. Place whole blanched almond on either side. Serve immediately.

CHERRY JUBILEE SUNDAE

If you like cherries you'll love this! Spicy cherries and cherry liqueur served hot over ice cream. Easy to make and easy to eat.

INGREDIENTS

½ 1-pound can cherry pie filling, thickened

1 or 2 sticks cinnamon, depending on size

6 whole cloves or ¼ teaspoon ground cloves

1 teaspoon frozen orange juice

¼ cup Cherry Heering or similar sweet liqueur

2 large scoops vanilla ice cream

ASSEMBLE

1 large pan

1 can opener

1 tablespoon

1 set measuring spoons

1 measuring cup

silver dishes

DIRECTIONS

Pour cherry pie filling, cinnamon, cloves, and orange juice into a pan. Add the Cherry Heering and bring to a boil, stirring constantly. Scoop the ice cream into individual dishes and top with the hot cherries. Serve immediately. This can be made in a chafing dish.

STRAWBERRY TRIFLE*

*A dessert the English hold dear . . . and little wonder!
This mellow blending of strawberries, cake, and vanilla
cream couldn't be more delicious.*

INGREDIENTS

- 1 3½-ounce package vanilla instant pudding
- 2 cups light cream
- 1 10-ounce package frozen strawberries in syrup, defrosted
- 1 package lady fingers
- 4 tablespoons sherry
- 20 fresh whole strawberries
- 1 can instant whipped cream (or fresh whipped if you have an extra minute)

ASSEMBLE

- 1 mixing bowl
- 1 rotary beater
- 1 set measuring spoons
- 1 measuring cup
- 1 paring knife
- 1 spoon
- 1 glass serving dish

DIRECTIONS

Place 2 cups light cream in mixing bowl. Add one box instant
vanilla pudding. Beat with rotary beater until pudding begins
to thicken. Line sides and bottom of serving dish with ½ thickness of lady fingers. Sprinkle with 2 tablespoons sherry. Cut
10 strawberries into thin slices. Spoon a layer of frozen strawberries and syrup onto lady fingers in bottom of dish. Cover
with fresh strawberry slices. Spread a layer of instant pudding
over strawberries and continue to fill serving dish with alternate
layers of lady fingers (sprinkled with sherry), strawberries in
syrup, fresh strawberries, and pudding until dish is filled. End
with layer of pudding.

NOTE

Serves 2 to bursting, 3 amply.

GARNISH

Cut 9 strawberries into quarters. Place remaining whole straw-berry in center of trifle. Decorate top of serving dish neatly with remaining pieces of strawberry. Pipe small points of whipped cream around strawberries. Place one fresh mint leaf on either side of whole strawberry. Serve immediately.

* May be prepared 24 hours in advance. Refrigerate until needed.

GREEK PONTICA

Yummy little fried cakes, as warm and golden as the Greek sun, served all crispy and tempting under a blanket of honey and pistachio nuts.

INGREDIENTS

4 slices white bread
1 egg
1 tablespoon milk
½ cup bread crumbs
5 tablespoons butter
6 tablespoons honey
1 package shelled pistachio nuts

ASSEMBLE

1 chafing dish
1 round cookie cutter or glass
1 shallow bowl for beaten egg
2 small bowls for honey and nuts
1 plate for fried bread rounds
1 set measuring spoons
1 large skillet
1 measuring cup
1 rolling pin
serving plates
Sterno

DIRECTIONS

Cut bread into rounds using cookie cutter. Crush shelled nuts with rolling pin. Place in small bowl. Measure honey into small bowl. Beat egg and milk in shallow bowl. Measure bread crumbs into plate. Measure one tablespoon butter into blazer pan. Place chafing dish and dishes containing nuts and honey on a tray ready for cooking at table. Meanwhile dip bread rounds quickly in egg and then in bread crumbs, and fry them in skillet containing the remaining butter. If not using chafing dish simply spoon one tablespoon honey and nuts over bread rounds and serve. Otherwise place fried bread rounds on tray until serving time. When ready to serve dessert carry tray and chafing dish to table. Light Sterno under blazer pan and warm fried bread rounds in the melted butter. Place bread rounds on plates, cover each with a tablespoon of honey and sprinkle with chopped pistachio nuts. Serve warm.

NOTE

More honey may be used if desired.

APPLE PANCAKE

This is a dish you will whip up not only for dessert but also for lunch, for Sunday brunch, on the spur of the moment for your late-hour guests. Not only good but authentic. Try it as soon as possible. You won't be sorry.

INGREDIENTS

¼ cup all purpose flour
2 tablespoons sugar
1 egg, beaten
2 teaspoons melted butter or vegetable oil
½ cup light cream
¼ teaspoon cinnamon
1 apple, peeled and thinly sliced
1 teaspoon prepared lime juice
2 tablespoons butter

ASSEMBLE

1 mixing bowl
2 measuring cups
1 set measuring spoons
1 fork
1 paring knife
10-inch flameproof skillet
1 pancake turner
serving plates

DIRECTIONS

Set oven at broil. Mix together flour and sugar. Beat egg, light cream, and melted shortening. Add liquid mixture to dry ingredients. Mix well. Melt one tablespoon butter in skillet. Pour in pancake batter. Cook until golden brown over medium heat. Do not turn. Meanwhile peel and slice apple into ¼-inch slices. Arrange apple on uncooked top of pancake. Sprinkle with one tablespoon sugar and ¼ teaspoon cinnamon. Dot with remainder of butter. Cook for 2 minutes under broiler, being careful not to burn. Remove from flame and fold carefully with pancake turner. Take care not to break. Sprinkle with a few grains of sugar and the lime juice. Cut and serve warm.

SHERBET IN ORANGE CUPS

A beautiful way to serve sherbet. The orange itself be-comes the serving dish. More than a dessert—a conver-sation piece.

INGREDIENTS

2 small scoops pineapple sherbet. If not available use lemon sherbet.

2 large scoops orange sherbet

2 large thick skinned oranges

4 fresh mint leaves

2 cumquats

ASSEMBLE

1 large ice cream scoop

1 small ice cream scoop

1 paring knife

DIRECTIONS

Cut through the rind only around the middle equator of one orange. Be careful not to cut into the orange itself. Gently loosen skin with tip of knife. Carefully pull half of the rind up to form a cup at the top of the orange. This cup should still be attached to the orange itself. Now carefully pull down the other half of the orange rind to form another cup at the bottom of the orange. This too should remain attached to the orange. Stand on end. Pull off any strings of white that may be on the cup or orange. Repeat process with other orange. In the open orange skin cup put a large scoop of orange sherbet. Top this with a small scoop of pineapple sherbet. Place the cumquat on top of this with a mint leaf on either side. Serve very cold.

CRÊPES SUZETTE

Again traditional. Again French. Again delicious. A famous dessert that deserves its fame. Thin little pancakes, with orange-brandy sauce, deliciously simple. Simply etc.

INGREDIENTS

½ cup sifted flour
¼ teaspoon salt
½ cup milk
1 egg
NOTE: 1 can plain crêpes may be substituted for the above if desired
2 tablespoons butter
¼ cup Cointreau
¼ cup brandy
4 teaspoons powdered sugar
1 orange
¼ cup butter

ASSEMBLE

1 mixing bowl
1 rotary beater
1 grater
2 tablespoons
1 set measuring spoons
1 measuring cup
1 griddle or skillet
1 chafing dish or skillet
1 box matches
serving plates

DIRECTIONS

In the mixing bowl beat the egg with rotary beater. Add half cup milk, flour, and salt and quickly beat with beater until batter is smooth. Grease griddle with 2 tablespoons butter and bake 6 three-inch pancakes or crêpes over medium high flame. Fold the crêpes in half and then in half again. Turn off the flame under griddle but leave crêpes on griddle to keep warm. Melt ¼ cup butter in blazer pan of a chafing dish or skillet. When butter begins to bubble add the folded crêpes and sprinkle each with a teaspoonful of the powdered sugar. Cut orange in half. When the crêpes are hot, squeeze the orange juice into the

pan. Add the Cointreau to the juice and spoon this sauce over the crêpes until they are thoroughly soaked through. Pour brandy over the top of the crêpes and light with a match. It will light easily after the brandy is slightly warmed by the hot crêpes. As soon as the brandy stops flaming, place 3 crêpes on each serving plate. Spoon a little of the remaining sauce over each crêpe. Serve immediately.

COLD OLD GERMAN FRUIT SOUP IN CANTALOUPE SHELLS*

Oom Pah Pah! Try this one for a cool and filling start or finish to a light meal or lunch. Zesty orange and cherry flavors in a spice-spiked soup. And you can eat the bowl.

INGREDIENTS

- 1 1-pound can cold cherry pie filling, thickened
- ½ cup cold orange juice
- 1 teaspoon cinnamon
- 1 generous pinch powdered cloves
- 2 whole sticks cinnamon
- 1 cantaloupe melon
- 1 can instant whipped cream

ASSEMBLE

- 1 blender
- 1 measuring cup
- 1 paring knife
- 1 spoon
- 1 can opener

DIRECTIONS

Pare the rind carefully from one whole cantaloupe. Slice the melon neatly in half. Remove pulp, seeds, and enough melon from center to hold soup. Place one can cherry pie filling, one teaspoon ground cinnamon, one pinch cloves, and ½ cup orange juice in blender. Blend on high speed for one minute or until smooth. Pour cherry orange mixture into cantaloupe shells. Decorate each with stick cinnamon.

GARNISH

Place a flowerlet of whipped cream in the center of the soup and decorate the edge of the melon with whipped cream also. Serve immediately.

* Soup may be prepared a day in advance and refrigerated until needed. Do not peel melon until serving time. Stir soup well before pouring into melon shells. Garnish immediately.

MOUSSE AU CHOCOLAT

Here is a dessert that promises to satisfy the most deep-rooted chocolate addiction. It's smooth, rich, and delectable. You won't believe anything so good can be so easy to prepare.

INGREDIENTS
½ 4½-ounce box chocolate instant pudding
½ cup heavy cream
½ cup light cream
½ cup instant whipped cream, canned
shavings of semisweet chocolate

ASSEMBLE
1 mixing bowl
1 electric mixer: the hand variety is best
1 measuring cup
1 slotted spoon
4 small earthenware pots

DIRECTIONS
Measure ½ cup light cream and ½ cup heavy cream into mixing bowl. Add ½ box instant pudding mix. Beat with hand mixer on slow or stir rapidly with spoon until mix thickens. Squirt approximately ½ cup of canned whipped cream onto instant pudding. With slotted spoon fold in whipped cream by cutting through cream, down into the pudding, then up and over, repeating process until the cream and the pudding are almost but not completely mixed. *Never stir!* Spoon mousse into the small earthenware pots, cut shavings of semisweet chocolate onto mousse. Refrigerate until serving time.

GARNISH
Top with ½ candied cherry and 2 pieces candied citron in the shape of a flower with leaves.

Drinks

Stir in friendship and serve

These drinks are in a category all by themselves. Each in its own way is special. The emphasis is not on alcoholic content: those recipes can be found in any bartender's guide. These are drinks with that certain flair that proves you care enough about your guests to go out of your way to please them. And how better to do that than by sharing their company over a delicious drink?

In every age, in every part of the world, even in the most primitive of civilizations the warmth of friendship has been considerably heightened by the glow produced from the favorite local brew. Whether it has been made on the sly in the Kentucky hills, filtered through charcoal in the shadow of the Kremlin, or chewed up in some witch-doctor's hut, the most important ingredient is not alcohol but camaradarie.

So it is with the drinks featured here. Hot Buttered Rum and Cider with Spiced Peach, warming when shared with friends after skiing. Cold Brandied Coffee with Ice Cream, cooling when sipped with fellow tennis enthusiasts after the match. Golden Peach Eggnog, festive when toasting in the New Year. Café Diable, really luxurious as a finale for your favorite dinner guests, or Mocha Steamer for you to enjoy if you're a nonimbiber as I am.

Whether you live in an igloo in the Arctic, a Chateau on the Riviera, or reign supreme, a queen in your own kitchen, brew up one of these drink recipes, stir in a liberal amount of friendship, and serve. You won't go wrong.

Drinks for occasions

HOT BUTTERED CIDER

A treat for the grown-ups on Halloween, or any crisp autumn evening when cider is available.

INGREDIENTS

- 2 mugs hot cider
- 2 tablespoons Cointreau
- 8 tablespoons golden rum
- 4 teaspoons brown sugar
- 2 teaspoons sweet butter
- 2 sticks cinnamon
- ¼ teaspoon allspice
- ¼ teaspoon cloves

ASSEMBLE

- 2 mugs; pewter is best
- 1 saucepan
- 1 set measuring spoons

DIRECTIONS

Pour rum and brown sugar into saucepan. Warm and set aflame. When flame goes out, add remaining ingredients and heat to scalding. Pour into pewter mugs and serve steaming.

HOT BUTTERED RUM AND CIDER WITH SPICED PEACH

Shades of Captain Morgan! Wouldn't he have loved a cup of this to warm his cold heart on a wind-tossed winter's night? He might have favored a stronger potion of rum, though, and so might you. If so, please do.

INGREDIENTS

2 cups hot cider
8 tablespoons rum
2 tablespoons juice from spiced peaches
4 teaspoons maple syrup
2 teaspoons sweet butter
2 canned spiced peaches
2 cinnamon sticks
8 cloves
¼ teaspoon allspice
2 pieces of orange peel

ASSEMBLE

2 pewter mugs
1 saucepan
1 set measuring spoons
1 paring knife
1 spoon

DIRECTIONS

Warm 8 tablespoons rum in saucepan. Cut 2 three-inch strips of orange rind. Place one strip with one tablespoon warm rum in each pewter mug. Light. When flame goes out add 2 teaspoons maple syrup, one teaspoon butter, the spices, one tablespoon of the spiced peach syrup, the spiced peach, and the remaining rum to each pewter mug. Heat cider to scalding in saucepan and pour over the mixture in the mug. Stir. Serve scalding.

HOT WINE PUNCH

Celebrating the victory of your favorite football team? Cold in the bones from sitting in the stadium? Scratchy in the throat from screaming the team on? Need something to warm and soothe and start the conversation flowing? Serve this and then just try to get your guests to leave.

INGREDIENTS

½ bottle claret
1 tablespoon lemon juice
1 tablespoon sugar
1 cinnamon stick
10 whole cloves
1 cup water

ASSEMBLE

1 chafing dish or saucepan
Sterno
1 corkscrew
1 set measuring spoons
1 measuring cup

DIRECTIONS

Light flame under blazing pan of chafing dish or under saucepan. Add lemon juice, sugar, cinnamon stick, cloves, and water. Bring to boil. Pour in claret and slowly heat. Do not boil. Serve hot.

GOLDEN PEACH EGGNOG

Your guests as well as your holiday candles will be all aglow if you whip up this froth of creamy eggnog with mellow peach brandy and golden rum. Guzzle the eggnog alone, then gobble up the peaches with vanilla ice cream and eggnog sauce. Too good to be true even on Christmas.

INGREDIENTS

2 eggs
¼ cup sugar
¼ cup peach brandy
½ cup golden rum
½ cup cognac
1 cup cold milk
½ cup heavy cream
⅛ teaspoon nutmeg
2 sticks cinnamon
4 peach halves
1 can instant whipped cream

ASSEMBLE

1 punch bowl and cups
1 ladle
1 electric mixer; hand mixer is easiest
2 mixing bowls
1 fork
1 spoon
1 measuring cup
1 set measuring spoons
1 can opener
paper toweling
silver dishes

DIRECTIONS

Separate egg whites from egg yolks, putting yolks in one mixing bowl and whites in another. Beat the egg yolks with a fork until they are light and creamy. Add ¼ cup sugar and continue to mix for one minute. Put egg yolk mixture into punch bowl. Slowly add ¼ cup peach brandy, ½ cup rum, and ½ cup cognac. Beat the egg whites with the electric mixer until they are stiff. Stir one cup cold milk and ½ cup heavy cream into punch bowl. Open can of peach halves and drain. Place 4 halves on paper toweling to remove excess moisture. Fold egg whites into mixture in punch bowl. Slide peaches into bottom of punch bowl. Add stick cinnamon. Decorate top of eggnog with canned instant whipped cream. Sprinkle with nutmeg. Serve immediately. Serve the peach halves in small silver dishes with vanilla ice cream and eggnog sauce topped with whipped cream and nutmeg.

Coffee drinks

COLD BRANDIED COFFEE WITH ICE CREAM

Peach ice cream in iced coffee, spiked with peach brandy and topped with whipped cream! Better than an ice cream soda for quenching your summertime thirst.

INGREDIENTS

4 heaping teaspoons instant coffee
2 cups cold water
2 tablespoons peach brandy
2 scoops peach ice cream
2 tablespoons canned instant whipped cream
2 pinches instant coffee
2 maraschino cherries

ASSEMBLE

2 very tall glasses
2 soda spoons
2 straws
1 measuring cup
1 set measuring spoons
1 ice cream scoop

DIRECTIONS

Measure 2 teaspoons instant coffee into each glass. Add a little cold water. Stir. Add cold water to within 2 inches of the top of the glass. Stir. Add one tablespoon peach brandy and one scoop ice cream to each glass. Stir. Top with whipped cream. Sprinkle with a small pinch of dry instant coffee. Top with a cherry and serve immediately with a straw and a soda spoon.

IRISH COFFEE

This hearty drink may be called Irish Coffee but it belongs to the world and the world is a happier place for it. Even kissing the Blarney Stone couldn't make the conversation flow more freely than a round of this mixture of coffee and Irish whiskey.

INGREDIENTS

8 tablespoons of Irish whiskey
4 level teaspoons instant coffee
1½ cups boiling water
4 tablespoons instant canned
   whipped cream

ASSEMBLE

1 saucepan
1 measuring cup
1 set measuring spoons
2 Irish coffee cups

DIRECTIONS

Boil water. Place instant coffee, whiskey, and boiling water into saucepan. Sugar as desired. Stir. Pour into Irish coffee cups. Top each with two tablespoons whipped cream. Serve immediately.

ICED COFFEE AND RUM

Here's a long, cold something to drink, with good strong coffee to pep you up so you're ambitious, and good smooth rum so you don't care whether you are or not. All in all it's the ideal hot weather drink.

INGREDIENTS

½ cup boiling water
1 cup cold water
8 ice cubes
2 tablespoons instant coffee
4 tablespoons rum
2 teaspoons sugar
¼ teaspoon nutmeg
1 can instant whipped cream

ASSEMBLE

saucepan
2 tall glasses
1 set measuring spoons
1 measuring cup
1 tablespoon

DIRECTIONS

Bring ½ cup water to boil in saucepan. Stir in instant coffee, one cup cold water, sugar, and rum. Put 4 ice cubes in each glass. Pour coffee mixture over ice so that one inch is left empty at the top of the glass. Top each with whipped cream and sprinkle with nutmeg. Serve cold.

CAFÉ DIABLE

Here's an instance where the drink can be the show stopper of the meal! Spicy black coffee with orange peel and cloves set aflame with ½ cup brandy. The devil with caution! Serve Café Diable.

INGREDIENTS

3 teaspoons instant coffee
3 cups boiling water
½ cup brandy
6 lumps sugar
thin outer peels of orange and lemon, which should be as long as possible
10 whole cloves
1 stick cinnamon

ASSEMBLE

1 chafing dish
Sterno
1 set measuring spoons
1 measuring cup
1 spoon
2 matches
1 ladle
1 quart bowl or coffee pot
2 demitasse cups

DIRECTIONS

Stick whole cloves through the lemon and orange peels at one-inch intervals. Light alcohol burner under chafing dish. Mix instant coffee and hot water in bowl or coffee pot. Heat brandy, orange and lemon peels with cloves, cinnamon, and 5 lumps of sugar in chafing dish until sugar is dissolved. Stir occasionally. Heat bowl of ladle over a match or low flame. Dip up a little of the mixture in the ladle. Put one lump of sugar in the ladle and light. Lower flaming ladle into the mixture in the chafing dish. While this is flaming, pour the hot coffee into chafing dish. When flame goes out, ladle coffee into demitasse cups. Serve hot.

MOCHA STEAMER

If you don't indulge in alcohol and you're tired of watching everyone else sipping something delicious while you sit sipless, stir up a Mocha Steamer and let your guests be jealous.

INGREDIENTS

8 level teaspoonfuls instant hot chocolate
2 level teaspoons instant coffee
8 tablespoons boiling water
1½ cups hot milk
4 tablespoons instant whipped cream, canned
¼ teaspoon chocolate sprinkles, optional

ASSEMBLE

2 coffee mugs
1 set measuring spoons
1 measuring cup
1 saucepan, small
1 teaspoon

DIRECTIONS

Light flame under tea kettle and boil a little bit of water. Place 4 level teaspoonfuls instant hot chocolate and 1 level teaspoonful instant coffee in each coffee mug. Add 4 tablespoonfuls boiling water to each cup. Stir. Pour the milk into the saucepan. Place over flame. When hot, pour ¾ cup into each mug. Stir. Top each with 2 tablespoons whipped cream. Sprinkle with chocolate sprinkles. Serve immediately.

Lunches, brunches, and midnight snacks

So much for dinner in all its ordered splendor. You're the acknowledged master (or mistress) of shopping, cooking, cleaning, dressing, and hostessing for the perfect dinner party, but what about those unusual or unanticipated occasions that cry out for a treatment of their own? Perhaps it's lunch for unexpected guests "just passing through around meal time," or lunch for that favorite aunt who is in town for a few days and who dotes on your cooking, or a snack for those late, late guests to whom you would like to serve something special, or perhaps just something yummy for yourself when you get hungry at some off-beat hour.

A good rule to remember is that recipes for lunches, brunches, or midnight snacks should be filling but not too heavy, impressive but not too grand. In general, lunches should be more delicate and underdone, midnight snacks more substantial and flamboyant, and brunches more wholesome, crackling with wake-up flavor and satisfying enough to take the place of the two light meals they replace, breakfast and lunch.

While lunches, brunches, and midnight snacks may seem tricky and unmanageable, especially when combined with the element of surprise, with proper planning they can be doubly rewarding because of the built-in relaxation supplied by the unusual hour and circumstances of their serving.

CREAMY SCRAMBLED EGGS WITH TRUFFLES

An exquisite combination is creamy scrambled eggs with truffles. Serve with champagne for a brunch or midnight supper that won't soon be forgotten.

INGREDIENTS

4 tablespoons sweet butter
2 tablespoons heavy cream
4 eggs
2 truffles diced
a sprinkle of white pepper and salt

ASSEMBLE

1 chafing dish (or heavy frying pan)
1 mixing bowl
1 fork
1 paring knife
1 set measuring spoons
1 can opener

DIRECTIONS

In blazer pan of a chafing dish or in the heavy frying pan place the butter. Turn flame on low. Open the can of truffles and chop two of them. Add the truffles to the butter. Meanwhile beat the eggs thoroughly in the mixing bowl. Add the beaten eggs, the juice from the can of truffles, and the heavy cream to the chafing dish. Stir constantly until eggs are firm but creamy. Never cook eggs until dry. Serve immediately.

GARNISH (*Optional*)

Slice one truffle in thin slices. Form a flowerlike pattern on the top of the eggs with these slices. Place a cherry tomato in the center of the flower.

EGGS WITH CHERRY TOMATOES

Not pretentious but really good is the recipe for a marvelous brunch or a special treat breakfast. Grilled cherry tomatoes and eggs set on a buttery mound of crumbs make a really toothsome treat.

INGREDIENTS

8 cherry tomatoes
2 eggs
2 pats butter
2 tablespoons breadcrumbs
2 pinches thyme
salt and pepper to taste

ASSEMBLE

2 small, individual flameproof
   dishes
1 paring knife
1 set measuring spoons

DIRECTIONS

Set broiler on high flame. Wash and dry tomatoes. Slice in half. Arrange tomato halves around edge of 2 flameproof dishes. Place pat of butter in center of each dish. Place under broiler flame for one minute. Remove dishes and sprinkle breadcrumbs in bottom of each. Break one egg over breadcrumbs in each dish. Sprinkle with thyme, salt, and pepper. Place under broiler until eggs set. Serve hot.

ASPARAGUS AND EGG WITH CHEDDAR CHEESE

Want a recipe for a delectable lunch? Stop here. Tender asparagus spears, fried eggs, and zesty Cheddar cheese combine for a lunch that will soothe the grouchiest guest.

INGREDIENTS

- 1 10-ounce package frozen asparagus
- 6 tablespoons butter
- 2 eggs
- 2 tablespoons grated Cheddar cheese
- 4 strips pimento

ASSEMBLE

- 1 small saucepan
- 1 set measuring spoons
- 1 medium size skillet
- 1 cover for skillet (or aluminum foil)
- 1 paring knife
- 2 oblong serving dishes

DIRECTIONS

Cook asparagus according to directions on package. Meanwhile, place butter in skillet. Carefully break two eggs into melted butter. Try to keep eggs from running together. Cover skillet. Cook over low heat. Drain asparagus, taking care not to break spears. Arrange asparagus neatly, ½ of the asparagus on each serving plate. Slide fried egg carefully onto each pile of asparagus.

GARNISH

Criss-cross egg yolks with pimento strips. Pour over the eggs and asparagus melted butter remaining in the skillet. Sprinkle each dish with one tablespoon of grated cheese. Serve immediately.

EGGS FLORENTINE

*An egg dish fit for a King. Spinach and poached eggs
topped with grated Swiss cheese and popped in the oven
for that one moment that makes the difference.*

INGREDIENTS

1 10-ounce package chopped
   frozen spinach
4 eggs
⅓ cup heavy cream
8 drops onion juice
3 tablespoons butter
2 tablespoons flour
1 cup milk
2 egg yolks
a dash of nutmeg
3 tablespoons grated Swiss or
   Cheddar cheese

ASSEMBLE

1 saucepan
1 small skillet
1 egg poacher
1 measuring cup
1 set measuring spoons
1 fork
1 spoon
1 small bowl
1 grater
2 individual baking dishes

DIRECTIONS

Set broiler on high flame. In saucepan cook frozen spinach
according to directions. Meanwhile poach eggs. In skillet melt
butter and stir in flour. Add milk and onion juice and stir until
sauce thickens. Beat 2 egg yolks and 2 tablespoons heavy cream
in the small bowl. Stir into sauce. Cook over very low flame.
Drain spinach and return to saucepan. Add remaining heavy
cream and nutmeg. Stir. Cover the bottoms of the two baking
dishes with the spinach mixture. Place two poached eggs in
each dish and cover each with half of the sauce in the skillet.
Sprinkle with grated Swiss cheese and place under broiler until
cheese melts and begins to brown. Serve very hot.

SWISS FONDUE

Do as the Swiss do and invite all your friends to dip a piece of crusty roll into this delectable "dunk." The delicate flavors of Swiss cheese, white wine, and cognac literally melt together to form one of the zestiest of late night snacks.

INGREDIENTS

¼ pound grated Swiss cheese
¾ teaspoon flour
½ teaspoon garlic powder
½ cup light dry white wine
2 tablespoons cognac or applejack
¼ teaspoon nutmeg
a dash each of salt and white pepper
2 hard rolls

ASSEMBLE

1 chafing dish
Sterno
1 measuring cup
1 set measuring spoons
1 paring knife
3 forks
1 bread basket lined with a napkin

DIRECTIONS

Light fire under blazer pan of chafing dish. Add wine, garlic powder and flour to the blazer pan. Do not boil. Merely heat to the boiling point. With a fork begin to stir the wine as you add the grated cheese a small handful at a time. Each handful of cheese must be completely melted before you add another. When all the cheese is melted and the mixture begins to bubble a little, add the nutmeg, salt, pepper, and cognac or applejack. Stir. Reduce heat to low and keep mixture warm without burning. Meanwhile cut the rolls into bite size pieces. Each piece of roll should have some crust on it. Serve at once in chafing dish. Dip pieces of roll in mixture. Eat at once.

SAUTÉED PÂTÉ DE FOIE GRAS AND SWISS CHEESE SANDWICHES

Rich, golden sautéed sandwiches filled with pâté de foie gras and melted Swiss cheese, topped with a smooth cheese sauce. Makes an appetizing lunch or late night snack.

INGREDIENTS

4 slices white bread
2 slices pâté de foie gras (canned)
1 cup grated Swiss cheese, packaged
2 tablespoons heavy cream
5 tablespoons butter
4 tablespoons olive oil
¼ cup white wine
½ cup heavy cream
½ cup chicken soup
1 egg yolk
1 egg
1 cup fine breadcrumbs, packaged
1 pinch nutmeg

ASSEMBLE

1 large skillet
1 small bowl
1 measuring cup
1 plate
1 set measuring spoons
1 knife
1 egg beater
1 round cookie cutter, 3 inches in diameter
2 serving plates

DIRECTIONS

Place 4 tablespoons olive oil and 4 tablespoons butter in skillet. Melt over low heat. Meanwhile cut 4 bread slices into rounds with cookie cutter. Cut 2 slices pâté de foie gras. Place on 2 bread rounds. Spread slightly. Measure ½ cup grated Swiss cheese into small bowl with one tablespoon butter and 2 tablespoons heavy cream. Mash together with spoon. Spread Swiss cheese mixture on remaining 2 bread rounds. Make sandwiches by placing together one cheese-spread bread round and one pâté-spread bread round. Beat egg in bowl and place bread crumbs on plate. Dip sandwiches first in beaten egg, then in bread crumbs, and sauté in butter and oil over medium heat until golden brown. Turn once. Place on serving plates. Mix together in skillet ½ cup concentrated cream of chicken soup, ¼ cup white wine, ½ cup of cream, ½ cup grated Swiss cheese, and nutmeg. Stir over medium heat. Meanwhile beat one egg yolk in small bowl. Add 2 tablespoons sauce to egg yolk. Stir. Over a low flame gradually add the egg yolk mixture to the sauce. Stir. Spoon over sandwiches. Serve sandwiches hot with cheese sauce.

LOBSTER À LA NEWBURG

There are few fine restaurants that do not feature this gourmet favorite. Too few home cooks do, but now it's easy! For that special treat, serve savory lobster this tried and true way.

INGREDIENTS

1 pound cooked lobster meat, fully defrosted
¼ cup sherry
½ cup heavy cream
2 tablespoons butter
2 egg yolks
¼ teaspoon flour
¼ teaspoon paprika
1 tablespoon cognac
2 slices toast

ASSEMBLE

1 skillet
1 butcher knife
1 measuring cup
1 set measuring spoons
1 mixing bowl
1 egg beater
1 tablespoon

DIRECTIONS

Slice lobster meat into ½-inch slices. Place butter in skillet. When butter is melted add lobster meat, ¼ cup sherry, ¼ teaspoon flour, and ¼ teaspoon paprika. Cook over high heat and stir constantly until sherry is reduced to half its original quantity. Turn flame to low. Separate whites from yolks of eggs. In mixing bowl beat egg yolks and cream. Pour over lobster meat. Stir until sauce begins to thicken. Do not boil. Add cognac. Cook 30 seconds more. Serve on toast points.

LOBSTER STEW

Try a bowl of this steaming stew as a special treat just for you. Pure ivory cream floats pieces of red-orange lobster meat, golden butter, black pepper, gray-green thyme, and paprika to make a treat for the eye as well as the palate.

INGREDIENTS

1 pound ready cooked lobster meat, fully defrosted
¾ cup clam juice
4 tablespoons butter
2 cups milk
1 egg yolk
½ cup heavy cream
½ teaspoon paprika
a dash or two of coarsely ground black pepper
2 pinches thyme
4 drops onion juice
2 tablespoons butter

ASSEMBLE

1 chafing dish (2 quart size)
Sterno
1 set measuring spoons
1 measuring cup
1 small mixing bowl
1 tablespoon
1 fork
2 large soup plates

DIRECTIONS

Place 4 tablespoons butter, 1 pound lobster meat and 4 drops onion juice in blazer pan of chafing dish. Light flame under blazer pan and cook lobster meat for one minute. Pour clam juice and milk over lobster. Stir. In a small bowl beat the egg yolk and heavy cream together. Gradually add the egg and cream mixture to the blazer pan of the chafing dish, stirring constantly. Add onion juice. Do not boil. Sprinkle with paprika, thyme and pepper. Serve immediately with chunks of lobster meat and liquid in each plate. Dot each plate of soup with one tablespoon butter.

WELSH RAREBIT
(Rabbit) with anchovies

A creamy combination of melted cheese, dry mustard, beer, and Worcestershire sauce, tawny and delicious. Spoon over toast points, garnish with tomato slices crisscrossed with anchovies, and slide under the broiler for a minute before serving. Made to order for lunches, brunches, or midnight snacks.

INGREDIENTS

¾ cup grated Cheddar cheese
2 tablespoons butter
1 cup beer
¼ teaspoon dry mustard
4 drops Tabasco sauce
1½ teaspoons Worcestershire
   sauce
2 slices tomato
4 pieces bread
2 sprinkles paprika
2 strips anchovy

ASSEMBLE

1 heavy skillet
1 set measuring spoons
1 measuring cup
1 toaster
1 spoon
1 paring knife
2 individual shallow baking
   dishes

DIRECTIONS

Turn broiler on high. Melt butter in skillet. Add one cup beer, 1½ teaspoons Worcestershire sauce, ¼ teaspoon dry mustard, 4 drops Tabasco sauce, and ¾ cup grated cheese. Stir. Turn flame to low. Make four slices toast. Cut toast into strips. Stir cheese and continue to cook until cheese is melted and sauce is smooth. Pile 6 toast strips on each baking dish, 3 going one way and 3 going the other. Pour welsh rarebit over toast.

GARNISH

Top each rarebit with a tomato slice criss-crossed with anchovy fillets. Sprinkle with paprika. Place under the broiler for one minute. Serve at once.

CREAMED CRAB MEAT AND OYSTERS

If any single dish approaches the perfection of the fabled ambrosia, this one does. You simply won't believe how luscious this is until you try it.

INGREDIENTS

½ cup crab meat or frozen king crab meat, fully defrosted

12 fresh shucked oysters, available at your fish store, or 1 7-ounce can frozen oysters, fully defrosted

¼ cup chicken consommé

3 tablespoons flour

6 tablespoons butter

1 cup milk

4 tablespoons heavy cream

14 stuffed olives

½ cup grated Cheddar or Swiss cheese, packaged

1 egg yolk

¼ teaspoon parsley flakes

ASSEMBLE

2 medium size skillets

1 set measuring spoons

1 measuring cup

1 small mixing bowl

1 egg beater

1 tablespoon

2 individual size ovenproof serving dishes

DIRECTIONS

Turn broiler on high flame. Melt 6 tablespoons butter in skillet. Add 3 tablespoons flour, ¼ teaspoon parsley flakes, one cup milk, and ½ cup grated cheese. Stir until smooth. Meanwhile place ¼ cup chicken consommé in the other skillet. Feel through oysters for bits of shells. Place oysters in skillet with chicken consommé. Heat for one minute. Stir. Cut ½ cup crab meat into small pieces. Gently stir oysters and crabmeat into cheese mixture in other skillet. Beat one egg yolk with 4 tablespoons heavy cream. Stir into sauce. Heat, being very careful not to boil. Divide equally in individual ovenproof dishes. Place stuffed olives at 2-inch intervals around edge of dish. Place under broiler until top is golden and beginning to brown here and there. Serve immediately.

GARNISH (*Optional*)

Butter 2 slices of toast. Cut off crusts and cut into eighths. Place toast with points up beside each olive around edge of dish. Tuck bits of parsley at the base of each bit of toast. Serve immediately.

Cooking out gourmet style

What is so disappointing as a backyard barbecue gone wrong? Steak, burned on the outside, still frozen on the inside. Hamburgers falling apart and covered with ashes. Baked beans straight from the can and tepid watermelon with a drowned bee floating in the juice. Meals that most people wouldn't dream of serving indoors even for Monday night supper are often foisted on guests under the guise of barbecuing.

How different outdoor gourmet cooking! Juicy pink shrimp, succulent chicken livers, their natural flavors heightened by the delicate smoky taste that can be achieved only by charcoal cooking, showy Baked Butter and Pea Beans with Mushrooms and Bacon—all dressed up and ready to cook when your guests arrive, leaving you free to enjoy, in luxurious leisure, not only the company of your friends but your own delicious cooking.

BARBECUE SAUCE

You've never tasted pork chops or spare ribs at their very best until you've had them nestled under this piquant barbecue sauce. Try it on oven-baked chicken, pork chops, ham too.

INGREDIENTS

1 medium size onion, diced
2 tablespoons butter
1 teaspoon dry mustard
1 tablespoon Worcestershire sauce
1 teaspoon lemon juice
¼ cup tomato catsup
¼ cup brown sugar
½ teaspoon salt
4 tablespoons chopped frozen green pepper
4 drops hot sauce or Tabasco sauce

ASSEMBLE

1 paring knife
1 set measuring spoons
1 measuring cup
1 skillet

DIRECTIONS

Peel and chop onion. Place skillet over medium heat. Add butter, then all other ingredients. Stir while sauce boils for 2 minutes. Serve hot over meat or chicken.

SCALLOPS AND CHERRY TOMATOES EN BROCHETTE

Scallops never had it so good! An attractive way to serve an old standby. Tasty and delicious, with a savory charcoal taste.

INGREDIENTS

½ pound bay scallops
20 cherry tomatoes
¼ cup melted butter
¼ teaspoon garlic powder
¼ teaspoon salt
½ cup bread crumbs
½ cup grated Parmesan cheese

ASSEMBLE

1 skillet
1 strainer
paper toweling
1 measuring cup
1 set measuring spoons
2 small skewers
1 pastry brush

DIRECTIONS

Turn broiler on high. Wash the scallops in the strainer. Turn onto paper toweling. Cook scallops in butter for one minute. Add ½ cup grated Parmesan cheese to ½ cup bread crumbs. Roll scallops in cheese-breadcrumb mixture. Thread skewers alternately with the scallops and cherry tomatoes. Brush with butter in pan. Sprinkle with garlic powder and salt. Cook over hot charcoal fire until browned.

RED RELISH FOR HAMBURGERS*

The relish supreme. A sweet and pungent blending of flavors that give hamburgers and hot dogs an excitement they've never had. Whip up a batch and keep it on hand. A real family pleaser.

INGREDIENTS

1 cup chopped uncooked frozen onion
1 cup chopped uncooked frozen green pepper
1 cup chopped uncooked sweet red pepper
6 tablespoons butter
2 teaspoons dry mustard
3 tablespoons Worcestershire sauce
1 tablespoon lemon juice
¾ cup tomato catsup
¾ cup brown sugar
1 teaspoon salt
12 drops hot sauce or Tabasco sauce
10 whole cloves
1 stick cinnamon
¼ teaspoon ground cloves

ASSEMBLE

1 skillet
1 measuring cup
1 set measuring spoons
1 paring knife
1 tablespoon

DIRECTIONS

Peel and chop the red pepper. Put skillet on a medium flame. Add butter, red and green pepper, and onion. Stir for one minute. Add the rest of the ingredients and stir until the mixture has boiled for 3 minutes. Serve hot, or fix ahead of time and serve cold. Good either way.

* May be prepared a week in advance and served hot or cold at serving time.

BAKED BUTTER AND PEA BEANS WITH MUSHROOMS AND BACON

No beans ever come out of a can tasting like this! These baked beans have mushrooms and bacon, green pepper and onion, not to mention spices and maple syrup, mustard and catsup. Sound like too much fuss to make over a bean? Oh, but these are special!

INGREDIENTS

½ 15-ounce can baked pork and beans
½ 14-ounce can butter beans, drained
3 slices bacon
½ green pepper
½ onion
½ 3½-ounce can sliced mushrooms, drained
¼ cup catsup
⅛ cup mild yellow mustard
⅓ cup maple syrup
½ teaspoon orégano
4 whole cloves
1 bay leaf

ASSEMBLE

1 saucepan
1 can opener
1 paring knife
1 spoon
1 earthenware dish

DIRECTIONS

Open cans of baked beans, butter beans, and mushrooms. Drain butter beans and mushrooms. Cut bacon slices in half and put in saucepan. Cook over medium high heat. Meanwhile cut the center from one green pepper and cut into slices ½-inch wide. Peel

½ onion and slice. Place green pepper and onion slices in saucepan with bacon and cook until onion is beginning to glaze and bacon is cooked but not crisp. Add all other ingredients. Stir until hot. Serve in earthenware dish.

NOTE
In this instance you will find it much easier if you double recipe and freeze unused portion.

STEAK KEBOBS

The hit of the barbecue! Succulent, bite-size chunks of steak, skewered between tomato, onion, mushroom, and green pepper, and done to a turn over the hot coals of your barbecue pit, or under the broiler, come winter!

INGREDIENTS

1 two-pound sirloin or tenderloin steak; have butcher remove bone and fat
2 tomatoes
1 large onion
1 green pepper
1 3-ounce can mushroom caps
3 tablespoons olive oil
¼ teaspoon garlic powder

ASSEMBLE

1 pastry brush
1 butcher knife
1 can opener
2 skewers for barbecuing

DIRECTIONS

Cut steak into one-inch cubes, omitting fat and gristle. Cut tomatoes into quarters. Peel onion and cut into one-inch wedges. Wash green pepper, remove pulp, and cut into 6 pieces. Open mushrooms and drain. Thread skewers with alternate pieces of steak, green pepper, tomato, onion, and mushroom caps. Brush with olive oil, sprinkle with garlic powder, and place over hottest part of charcoal fire. Cook two or three minutes, turning frequently. Serve immediately.

PINEAPPLE, SHRIMP, CHICKEN LIVERS, AND OLIVES ON SKEWERS

A tempting hors d'oeuvre with enough variety to satisfy any number of guests. Just thread these tasty morsels alternately on skewers, brush with French dressing, sprinkle with nutmeg, and charcoal grill for barbecue cooking that's bound to please.

INGREDIENTS

6 canned pineapple chunks
6 chicken livers
6 large cooked shrimp
6 stuffed olives
¼ cup French dressing
ground nutmeg

ASSEMBLE

1 can opener
2 skewers
1 measuring cup
1 pastry brush

DIRECTIONS

Arrange shrimp, pineapple, chicken livers, and olives on skewers. Brush with French dressing. Sprinkle with ground nutmeg. Cook over charcoal fire until slightly brown. Serve immediately.

GINGER-SHRIMP KEBOBS*

There would be a shout heard round the world if every-one who loved shrimps stood up and hollered "I!" These shrimps embellished with ginger, garlic, and soy sauce will be deemed special even by seafood connoisseurs. Cook them now and hear the cheers.

INGREDIENTS

8 very large raw shrimp
1 red pepper
1 green pepper
½ cup olive oil
1 teaspoon powdered ginger
1 teaspoon garlic powder
2 tablespoons soy sauce

ASSEMBLE

1 pair scissors
1 paring knife
1 mixing bowl
1 measuring cup
1 set measuring spoons
paper toweling
2 skewers

DIRECTIONS

Wash shrimps. Drain on paper toweling. Remove shell and vein from shrimp by making cut ¼-inch deep with scissors down en-tire back of shrimp. In mixing bowl place olive oil, powdered ginger, garlic powder, soy sauce, and shrimp. Stir to coat shell-fish thoroughly with sauce. Wash red and green peppers and discard seeds. Cut peppers into pieces one inch by 2 inches. Add to shrimp in bowl. Stir. Thread skewers first with red and green pepper strips, then with shrimp. Repeat until skewers are full or until seafood is used up. Broil over very hot charcoal fire basting with soy sauce mixture from time to time.

*May be prepared several hours in advance. Marinate seafood and red and green peppers in soy sauce mixture and thread on skewers just prior to cooking.

CHICKEN, PINEAPPLE, AND SWEET POTATO KEBOBS

Barbecue cooking shades of the Old South! These delectable kebobs bring together flavors that were meant for each other. Even the children will love them.

INGREDIENTS

10 chunks raw chicken meat
10 pineapple chunks
1 1-pound can whole sweet pota-
    toes
6 slices bacon
2 tablespoons butter
¼ cup maple syrup

ASSEMBLE

1 butcher knife
1 small pastry brush
2 skewers
1 can opener

DIRECTIONS

Cut chicken into one-inch chunks. Remove any skin. Drain sweet potatoes and cut into one-inch chunks. Cut bacon strips in half. Wrap 12 potato chunks in bacon. Alternately thread chicken, pineapple chunks, and bacon-wrapped sweet potatoes on skewers. Melt 2 tablespoons butter in saucepan. Add ¼ cup maple syrup. Brush skewered food with syrup mixture. Broil over most intense heat, basting with syrup from time to time. Turn skewers often. Serve hot.

NOTE

Equally good when cooked under the broiler of your kitchen stove.

CHICKEN LIVERS AND GRAPES

A new combination for barbecue cooking. Soft, pink, chicken livers charcoal broiled with white grapes. It's the brush with concentrated orange juice that makes them so delicious.

INGREDIENTS

10 chicken livers
20 white grapes
2 tablespoons concentrated frozen orange juice
1 tablespoon orégano

ASSEMBLE

1 colander
paper toweling
1 pastry brush
1 can opener
2 long skewers

DIRECTIONS

Wash chicken livers and grapes in colander. Put chicken livers on paper toweling to drain. Thread the skewers alternately with chicken livers and grapes. Brush livers and grapes with frozen orange juice concentrate. Sprinkle with orégano. Place over hottest part of charcoal fire. Turn almost constantly until livers are barely cooked. Serve hot and pink.

FRUIT EN BROCHETTE

Barbecued fruit, brushed with honey and set aflame with brandy: serve over vanilla, rum, or any fruit ice cream to culminate the perfect cookout.

INGREDIENTS

8 Maraschino cherries
10 chunks canned pineapple
2 fresh ripe peaches
4 fresh apricots
¼ cup honey
8 tablespoons fruit brandy

ASSEMBLE

2 small skewers
1 measuring cup
1 pastry brush
1 paring knife
1 bowl
paper towels

DIRECTIONS

Wash peaches and apricots. Peel peaches. Thread the fruit on the skewers, beginning and ending with a cherry. Place honey and brandy in bowl. Stir. Brush fruit with this mixture. Cook for a few minutes over charcoal fire. Remove fruit from fire once and brush again with honey-brandy mixture. When fruit is hot and beginning to brown here and there, remove from fire and dribble with brandy. Place skewers back on the fire to ignite the brandy. Serve flaming. Delicious served alone or over vanilla, rum, or any fruit ice cream.

Leftovers

Ugly ducklings turned to swans

Did you ever look at some particularly tempting bit of leftover food, swear that it was too good to discard, resolve to use it the following day, and instead find yourself throwing it away a few days later?

I'm sure you have and with very good reason. Food that is recooked is seldom very tasty. But there are exceptions to every rule and this rule is no exception. There are some foods that actually taste better when they are served the second day in some new, tempting way. But the way makes all the difference. The common method of serving leftover food is merely to reheat it, often without the benefit of even a sauce. If there is one thing cooked food doesn't need it is more cooking. Small wonder "leftovers" are most often limp and tasteless.

The secret of leftover cooking is very often no cooking at all, as in Asparagus Vinaigrette, Coquilles St. Jacques Salad, Eggs à la Russe, Cold String Bean and Shrimp Salad, Asparagus and Smoked Salmon Salad, or Vegetables à la Grecque. Here pre-cooked food is used as it would be if these recipes were started from scratch. These recipes *call* for cooked food. It's really not like using leftovers at all, so naturally these dishes turn out sparkling and still full of life. In Chicken Princesse and Breast of Chicken Perigourdine, chicken, which would tend to dry out if reheated in any other manner, is placed in a rich sauce and not cooked . . . just warmed enough to taste delicious. In the recipe for Potato Pflutters the food to be recooked takes an entirely different form and so does not taste tired and lifeless but retains the brightness and vitality of newly cooked foods. The recipes you find in this section may be based on those ugly ducklings of the kitchen, leftovers, but, true to form, at the end of the story those ugly ducklings turn into swans.

Leftover eggs

EGGS A LA RUSSE

Here's a classic found on the most distinguished menus. And so easy to prepare!

INGREDIENTS
2 leftover hard-cooked eggs
½ cup mayonnaise
2 tablespoons chili sauce
½ teaspoon tarragon vinegar
2 drops Tabasco sauce
10 drops lemon juice
2 teaspoons black caviar
2 teaspoons red caviar

ASSEMBLE
1 small mixing bowl
1 measuring cup
1 set measuring spoons
1 tablespoon
2 small serving plates

DIRECTIONS
Place mayonnaise, chili sauce, vinegar, Tabasco sauce, and lemon juice in mixing bowl. Stir. Peel hard-cooked eggs and cut in half lengthwise. Place 2 egg halves, yolks down, on each serving plate. Cover eggs with sauce. Top one egg half with one teaspoon black caviar, the other with red caviar. Serve cold.

Leftover chicken

BREAST OF CHICKEN PERIGOURDINE

One of the most esoteric of company dishes, using leftover chicken breast. Succulent white chicken meat enhanced with a rich brown Perigourdine sauce spiked with truffles, topped off with a slice of fine pâté de foie gras. Rich and unbelievably delicious!

INGREDIENTS

1 whole chicken breast, cooked
2 tablespoons chopped onion, uncooked
3 tablespoons butter
1 tablespoon flour
1 10½-ounce can consommé
3 tablespoons tomato sauce
2 tablespoons chopped black
   truffle
1 teaspoon truffle juice
3 tablespoons sherry
1 teaspoon meat extract
2 slices fine pâté de foie gras

ASSEMBLE

1 skillet
1 can opener
1 paring knife
1 set measuring spoons

DIRECTIONS

Carefully remove meat from bone, keeping breast meat in 2 whole pieces. If necessary, trim uneven edges from each half chicken breast. Place 3 tablespoons butter in skillet. Add chopped frozen onion. Brown onion *slightly*. Add one tablespoon flour. Stir. Cook until flour is *brown* but not burned. Add one can consommé and juice, 2 tablespoons chopped truffle, 3 tablespoons tomato sauce, 3 tablespoons sherry, one teaspoon meat extract, and 2 pieces of chicken breast. Boil over high flame for 3 or 4 minutes, stirring occasionally. Do not allow sauce to stick or burn. Place chicken breasts on plate. Top each with three spoons of sauce and one generous slice pâté de foie gras. Serve immediately with extra sauce served separately.

NOTE

To serve 4 double amounts of chicken and broccoli only.

WINE

Bordeaux Graves

CHICKEN PRINCESSE

I guarantee you won't have anything left over but the dish in which you cook this deliciously creamy treat, using left- over chicken and broccoli. If you have never tasted a Broccoli-Chicken recipe you had better hurry and make amends by cooking (and eating) this lovely Chicken Princesse.

INGREDIENTS	ASSEMBLE
1 cup leftover chicken meat, boned	1 blender
1 10½-ounce can cream of chick- en soup	1 can opener
4 tablespoons sherry	1 skillet
3 tablespoons heavy cream	1 set measuring spoons
1 cup leftover cooked broccoli	1 saucepan
¼ cup grated Swiss or Cheddar cheese, packaged	1 grater
10 whole packaged blanched al- monds	1 measuring cup
	1 fork
	paper towels
	1 shallow ovenproof serving dish
	1 spoon

DIRECTIONS

Set broiler flame on high. Open chicken soup and pour into blender. Blend for one minute on high speed. Pour into skillet. Add one cup chicken, 3 tablespoons cream, 4 tablespoons sherry, and heat. Place cooked (one cup) broccoli on paper toweling to drain for a second. Line bottom of flameproof dish with broccoli and chicken meat. Pour chicken soup mixture over broccoli and chicken. Sprinkle with blanched almonds and grated cheese. Place under broiler for one minute or until cheese is melted and slightly browned. Serve very hot.

NOTE

To serve 4 double amounts of chicken and broccoli only.

GARNISH (*Optional*)

Before placing under broiler squeeze one cup mashed potato mixed with 2 tablespoons each butter and heavy cream through pastry tube and pipe a ring around edge of dish. Place under broiler until golden brown and serve immediately.

WINE

Moselle, German Dry, slightly chilled

Leftover potatoes

BAKED STUFFED CHEESE POTATOES

If you think there's nothing less promising than a cold potato, these cheesy leftover baked potatoes may change your mind. They're perfect for any occasion. Delicious enough to serve to your guests, but not too exotic for your family's tastes, they're sure to become a speciality of your house.

INGREDIENTS

2 large leftover baked potatoes
2 cloves garlic
½ cup grated cheese
2 tablespoons grated Swiss or Cheddar cheese
6 tablespoons milk
2 tablespoons butter
½ teaspoon salt

ASSEMBLE

1 tablespoon
1 fork
1 garlic press
1 paring knife
1 electric hand mixer
1 set measuring spoons
1 tablespoon
1 large mixing bowl
1 measuring cup
1 small saucepan

DIRECTIONS

Set broiler on high flame. Cut a lengthwise slice from the top of each potato. Scoop out pulp, being careful not to damage potato shells. Peel and crush 2 garlic cloves. Place potato pulp, garlic pulp, ½ cup grated cheese, and the ½ teaspoon salt in the mixing bowl. Mash with fork until fairly smooth. Heat the 6 tablespoons milk and 2 tablespoons butter in saucepan. Add potato mixture to saucepan. Stir for one minute over high heat. Cream potatoes using hand mixer on high speed. Pile potato high into the potato shells. Press one tablespoon grated cheese onto top of each potato. Place under broiler for one minute. Serve hot.

CLAM HASH*

If you're the one who always says "Let's all come back to my place after," here's a wonderful dish using leftover boiled potatoes for an impromptu cold weather snack. The smoky taste of bacon and the clammy taste of clams seem to melt together with a perfection that's hard to believe until you taste it for yourself.

INGREDIENTS

1 7½-ounce can minced clams
3 strips bacon
¾ cup chopped onion, frozen, uncooked
3 medium size leftover boiled potatoes
2 teaspoons flour
2 teaspoons butter
2 teaspoons Worcestershire sauce
¼ teaspoon salt
¼ teaspoon pepper

ASSEMBLE

1 can opener
1 paring knife
1 measuring cup
1 set measuring spoons
1 skillet
1 cup
1 tablespoon
1 slotted spoon

DIRECTIONS

Cut 3 strips bacon in quarters and place in skillet. Place skillet over high heat. Fry bacon for one minute. Lower flame to medium, add onion, and cook until light brown. With slotted spoon place one can minced clams in skillet. Carefully pour remaining clam liquid into skillet, avoiding any sand which may be present in bottom of can. Peel and chop 3 potatoes. Add to clam mixture. Cook for one minute. Cream flour and 2 teaspoons butter in cup. Add butter mixture, 2 teaspoons

Worcestershire sauce, salt and pepper, to clam hash. Stir until slightly thickened and serve hot.

GARNISH (*Optional*)
Sprinkle with finely chopped parsley if desired.

* May be prepared several hours in advance if desired. Reheat at serving time.

COQUILLES ST. JACQUES SALAD

A salad out of the ordinary in its subtle combination of tastes, using leftover boiled potatoes and scallops, this definitely is something you should try if you tend to like the unusual rather than the flamboyant when it comes to food. Definitely understated. Definitely gourmet.

INGREDIENTS

2 small leftover potatoes, boiled in their jackets
1 cup cooked scallops
¾ cup white wine
¾ cup mayonnaise
1 egg yolk
1 teaspoon olive oil
4 drops onion juice, prepared
½ teaspoon lemon juice
2 tablespoons chopped frozen onion
1 tablespoon frozen chives

ASSEMBLE

1 small saucepan
1 paring knife
1 measuring cup
1 large mixing bowl
2 small mixing bowls
1 wire whisk or fork
1 set measuring spoons
1 salad bowl

DIRECTIONS

Bring ¾ cup of wine and 2 tablespoons chopped onion to a boil. Remove from flame. Peel and slice two small potatoes. Place sliced potatoes and one cup scallops in large mixing bowl. Pour warm wine and onion over them. In mixing bowl whisk one egg yolk until it is creamy. Add ¾ cup mayonnaise, one teaspoon olive oil, 4 drops onion juice, and ½ teaspoon lemon juice to egg yolk. Whisk until the mayonnaise is smooth. Drain potatoes and scallops. Mix potatoes and scallops with mayonnaise. Put salad into salad bowl and sprinkle with chives. Serve at room temperature.

POTATO PFLUTTERS

Bound to cause a flutter at dinner are these fluffy little potato pflutters, using leftover mashed potatoes. Puffy, golden brown, and just garlicky enough to please, they're sure to win over guests in a hurry—or try them as a special touch to a family meal! Even the children will love them.

INGREDIENTS

2 cups mashed potatoes
2 egg yolks
4 tablespoons hot melted butter
½ teaspoon salt
¼ teaspoon nutmeg
½ teaspoon garlic powder
4 teaspoons parsley flakes

ASSEMBLE

1 measuring cup
1 set measuring spoons
1 fork or electric mixer
1 spoon
1 mixing bowl
1 small sauce pan
1 ovenproof serving dish

DIRECTIONS

Turn broiler flame on high. Melt butter in saucepan. Mix potatoes, egg yolks, 4 tablespoons butter together with a fork or electric mixer. When fairly well mixed, add remaining ingredients and mix again. Place spoonfuls of the potato mixture on the greased serving dish and place under broiler for 5 minutes. Serve hot.

Leftover vegetables

ASPARAGUS AND SMOKED SALMON SALAD*

Not complicated but really good either as a salad or as an attractive addition to a cold dinner menu. Or better yet, make half a recipe and try it when you're lunching alone. Nothing's too good for you.

INGREDIENTS

4 slices smoked salmon, Alaska
    or Nova Scotia
12 stalks cold cooked leftover
    asparagus
4 strips pimento
4 thin wedges lemon
2 tablespoons tarragon vinegar
2 pinches of tarragon
¼ teaspoon salt

ASSEMBLE

1 paring knife
1 set measuring spoons
2 serving plates

DIRECTIONS

Place two slices smoked salmon side by side on serving plates. If the slices are narrow place them an inch or two apart so that

they will show under the asparagus. Place 3 spears of asparagus side by side on top of the slices of smoked salmon and facing the same direction. On top of the three spears of asparagus place two spears, then one. Repeat on second plate. Sprinkle each mound of asparagus with one tablespoon vinegar and a little salt.

GARNISH

Cut 4 thin wedges of lemon and 4 strips of pimento. Place one wedge of lemon on either side of the mounds of asparagus. Sprinkle with a pinch of tarragon. Form an X of pimento on each mound of asparagus. Serve cold.

* Can be prepared several hours in advance and refrigerated until needed.

SAUCE VINAIGRETTE FOR USE IN ASPARAGUS VINAIGRETTE*

There are few sauces as tasty as a good vinaigrette sauce, and this one is very good indeed. If you have never tried cold Asparagus Vinaigrette at home, and where the portions are large and just as you like them, do try! You have a treat in store.

INGREDIENTS
¼ cup tarragon vinegar
2½ tablespoons olive oil
2 teaspoons prepared lemon juice
3 teaspoons sugar
½ teaspoon salt
1 scallion
1 large dill pickle
2 tablespoons green pepper, frozen uncooked and chopped
1 hard-cooked egg
salt and pepper to taste

ASSEMBLE
1 measuring cup
1 set measuring spoons
1 paring knife
1 small mixing bowl
1 tablespoon

DIRECTIONS
Finely chop scallion, dill pickle, and hard-cooked egg. In mixing bowl blend vinegar, lemon juice, olive oil, salt and pepper, and sugar. Add all remaining ingredients. Serve cold.

*May be prepared 24 hours in advance of serving. Refrigerate until needed.

ASPARAGUS VINAIGRETTE*

INGREDIENTS

14 spears cold cooked asparagus
10 tablespoons Sauce Vinaigrette

ASSEMBLE

1 set measuring spoons
1 fork
2 small plates

DIRECTIONS

Arrange asparagus spears on two plates, four spears side by side, three on top of these. Pour 5 tablespoons Sauce Vinaigrette over each stack of asparagus. Serve cold.

GARNISH (*Optional*)

Cut one hard-cooked egg in slicer. Cut 4 long strips of pimento. Press one egg yolk through a fine sieve onto a paper napkin. Place slice of hard-cooked egg on the center of each mound of asparagus. Top each egg slice with teaspoon of sieved hard-cooked egg yolk. Top with one caper. Place one strip of pimento across the tips of the asparagus and one across base end. Repeat on second plate. Serve cold.

* May be prepared 24 hours in advance of serving. Refrigerate until needed.

SPINACH SALAD

Everyone knows hard-cooked eggs and spinach make a wonderful team, but if the spinach is uncooked and anchovies are added, the team becomes unbeatable. Try it and see for yourself.

INGREDIENTS

4 cups raw spinach leaves, loosely packed
8 anchovy fillets
2 leftover hard-cooked eggs, chopped
2 leftover hard-cooked eggs, cut in quarters
¼ cup prepared Italian dressing: 6 tablespoons olive oil and 3 tablespoons white wine vinegar may be substituted if desired
8 strips pimento

ASSEMBLE

1 colander
paper toweling
1 paring knife
1 measuring cup
1 salad bowl
2 salad plates

DIRECTIONS

Wash spinach thoroughly and remove stems. Drain in colander. Pat dry with paper towels. Break spinach leaves into bite size pieces and arrange in salad bowl. Drain anchovy fillets on a paper towel. Cut fillets into fourths and add to salad bowl. Pour dressing over salad. Toss. Serve cold.

GARNISH

Sprinkle with finely chopped, hard-cooked eggs. Arrange 8 quarters of hard-cooked eggs around edge of bowl, points toward center. Decorate each egg quarter with 1 small strip pimento. Serve cold.

COLD STRING BEAN AND SHRIMP SALAD*

Can't think of anything less interesting than a cold, cooked, leftover green bean? Before you condemn it you had better try it with cold cooked shrimp, hard-cooked eggs, and French dressing. You'll be ashamed you maligned that bean.

INGREDIENTS

1 cup leftover green beans, cold
8 large cold cooked shrimp, peeled and cleaned
4 hard-cooked eggs, cold
⅓ cup cold French dressing
7 black olives

ASSEMBLE

1 large mixing bowl
1 measuring cup
1 paring knife
1 sieve
1 salad fork and spoon
1 salad bowl

DIRECTIONS

Slice the shrimp in half lengthwise. Place the green beans and the shrimp in the mixing bowl. Halve the hard-cooked eggs and slice the whites into thin strips. Add the sliced egg whites and the French dressing to the shrimp and beans. Toss, and place in the salad bowl.

GARNISH

Put the egg yolks through a sieve, then sprinkle them over the salad as a garnish. Form a pinwheel of 5 shrimp in the center of the bowl, place one black olive in the center of the shrimp pinwheel and one in the curve of each shrimp used for decoration. Serve cold.

* May be prepared several hours early. Garnish immediately before serving.

VEGETABLES A LA GRECQUE*

Using leftover cauliflower, zucchini. (Green beans, mixed vegetables, lima beans may be substituted or added.) These sparkling bright cooked vegetables, served refreshingly cold are crisp, succulent, delicious, and guaranteed to please even the confirmed vegetable hater. A marvelous addition to Hors d'Oeuvre Varies or Hors d'Oeuvre tray.

INGREDIENTS

½ cup leftover cooked cauliflower
½ cup leftover zucchini
4 artichoke hearts (the smaller the better)
8 small white canned onions
1 3-ounce can mushroom caps
2 sprigs parsley
4 tablespoons olive oil
2 tablespoons lemon juice
2 cloves garlic
½ teaspoon salt
⅛ teaspoon black pepper
½ teaspoon dried and chopped chervil

ASSEMBLE

1 small mixing bowl
1 large mixing bowl
1 can opener
1 garlic press
1 paring knife
2 forks
paper toweling
1 serving plate

DIRECTIONS

All ingredients should be cold. Open cans or jars of white onions, mushroom caps and artichoke hearts. Drain all vegetables, measure, and place in large mixing bowl. Measure 4 tablespoons olive oil, 2 tablespoons lemon juice, ½ teaspoon salt, and ⅛ teaspoon black pepper into small mixing bowl. Peel garlic cloves. Crush in garlic press over bowl. Add to olive oil. Mix well. Pour olive oil mixture over vegetables. Toss lightly with 2 forks. Arrange on serving plate. Wash and chop parsley. Sprinkle parsley and ½ teaspoon dried chervil over salad. Serve cold.

NOTE

Serves 2 or 3.

* May be prepared 24 hours in advance and kept in refrigerator or until needed.

Sauces

"La sauce c'est tout"

If there is any one thing that separates the true gourmet cook from the heavy-handed chintz-and-ruffles housewife cook, it is the appreciation of sauces.

Now, don't let that frighten you away. You don't have to invent the sauces. You just have to understand them. Once you understand them you will appreciate them, and once you appreciate them, almost automatically you will be transformed into a gourmet cook. It sounds simple and it is meant to be.

The first thing to understand about gourmet sauces is this. With the exception of white sauces, they seldom use flour. Where thickening is desired it is nearly always obtained by using egg yolks or, in the case of meat sauces, by reduction in quantity through cooking.

Second, sauces, while of supreme importance in flavor, are invariably used sparingly.

Third, the gourmet sauce is subtle in flavor even at its richest.

It takes a practiced palate indeed to decipher the subtleties in a French sauce, but most often you can count on the following: (1) light sauce contains heavy cream, butter in quantity, white wine, brandy, veal or chicken stock, and those wizards, shallots. An onion can be substituted for shallots, but try to avoid this if you possibly can. Cook the same dish with onions and then with shallots and I guarantee you'll never again make the substitution if it is avoidable. (2) A golden sauce is a light sauce thickened with egg yolks. (3) A brown sauce nearly always contains meat juices, red or white wine, shallots, and parsley. (4) Basic white sauces contain milk, flour, butter, and salt.

Even the variations have their rules: Spanish sauces almost always contain olive oil, onion, tomato, green pepper, and garlic.

Creole sauces mimic French and Spanish sauces, but often with olives or okra added. Hawaiian sauces most often contain soy sauce, ginger, and pineapple.

In France (Sauce Heaven) they say, "La Sauce c'est tout"— "The Sauce is all." Whether it is an invisible cloak of flavor or lies in folds as rich and smooth as brown silk velvet, the truth is in the tasting. "La Sauce c'est tout!"

MEXICAN CURRY SAUCE

A wow of a sauce with more built-in "sit up and take notice" than a string of fire crackers. Serve this with left-over chicken, lamb, shrimp, crab meat, or hard-cooked eggs, add a little rice, and watch a 4-star meal appear out of almost nothing.

INGREDIENTS

3 tablespoons cooking oil
½ teaspoon salt
6 tablespoons frozen chopped on-
    ion, uncooked
¾ tablespoon curry powder
1 tablespoon flour
1 cup milk
6 tablespoons frozen chopped
    green pepper, uncooked
3 tablespoons chopped red pi-
    mento

ASSEMBLE

1 skillet
1 set measuring spoons
1 measuring cup
1 small saucepan
1 paring knife

DIRECTIONS

In a skillet heat 3 tablespoons cooking oil over medium high flame. Add 6 tablespoons chopped onions to the hot cooking oil. Cook onions until they are brown. Do not burn. Add ¾ tablespoon curry powder, one tablespoon flour and ½ teaspoon salt to the onions and stir. Pour one cup milk into the onion mixture. Stir rapidly until smooth. Chop 3 tablespoons pimento. Add green pepper and pimento to the curry sauce. Boil rapidly for 2 minutes. Serve with left-over chicken or meat (preferably lamb).

CREOLE SAUCE

No wonder Creole cooking is popular! A sauce like this can transform the plainest meat or poultry into a heavenly treat. If you can't get away for a trip to New Orleans, have a sip of this sauce instead. Try it on flounder or halibut or leftover chicken or pot roast. Equally good over all.

INGREDIENTS

2 tablespoons butter
3 tablespoons frozen, uncooked, chopped green pepper
3 tablespoons frozen uncooked chopped onion
10 mushrooms peeled and sliced or 1-ounce can sliced mushrooms (drained)
10 stuffed green olives, sliced
¼ cup beef consommé
¼ cup water
1 cup stewed tomatoes
¼ teaspoon garlic powder
1 tablespoon sherry
¼ teaspoon thyme
1 bay leaf

ASSEMBLE

1 skillet
1 set measuring spoons
1 paring knife
1 can opener
1 tablespoon
1 blender
1 strainer

DIRECTIONS

Place skillet over medium high flame. Add 2 tablespoons butter, 3 tablespoons each of chopped green peppers and onion. Sauté this while you peel and slice 10 mushrooms. Add mushrooms. Slice 10 olives into circles. Add olives, ¼ cup consommé, and ¼ cup water. Stir. Place one cup of stewed tomatoes in container of blender. Cover and blend on high speed for 30 seconds. Pour tomatoes through a strainer into the skillet. Stir with a spoon to force most of the tomatoes through the strainer. Add thyme, one bay leaf, ¼ teaspoon garlic powder, and one tablespoon sherry. Boil. Serve hot.

SAUCE MADRID

Here's a cold seafood sauce with enough zing to open any eye. As a special treat, marinate cooked shrimp in it overnight. Serve as one of a selection of cold hors d'oeuvres. Marvelous.

INGREDIENTS

½ cup olive oil
5 tablespoons wine vinegar
1 tablespoon lemon juice
3 tablespoons cognac
1 tablespoon chopped celery
1 tablespoon horseradish
1 tablespoon minced scallion
3 tablespoons chili sauce
2 teaspoons chopped chives
2 teaspoons chopped parsley
½ teaspoon dry mustard
1 egg yolk
a pinch each salt and pepper

ASSEMBLE

1 medium size mixing bowl
1 measuring cup
1 paring knife
1 set measuring spoons
1 wire whisk or slotted spoon

DIRECTIONS

Chop celery, scallion, and parsley fine. Place all ingredients in mixing bowl. Mix thoroughly with wire whisk or slotted spoon. Serve cold. Delicious over cold seafood, especially shrimp. Serve over Avocado and Shrimp Salad.

HAWAIIAN STEAK SAUCE

Tired of steak the same old way? Looking for a marinade that's really good? Here it is, with many thanks to the Islands for dreaming it up.

INGREDIENTS

- ⅓ cup soy sauce
- 2 cloves garlic
- ¼ teaspoon powdered ginger
- 2 pinches monosodium glutamate
- ¼ cup pineapple juice
- ½ teaspoon sugar

ASSEMBLE

- 1 mixing bowl
- 1 set measuring spoons
- 1 measuring cup
- 1 garlic press

DIRECTIONS

Stir all ingredients except garlic together in mixing bowl. Peel garlic and crush over mixing bowl. Scrape bottom of garlic press to obtain as much garlic as possible. Stir and use for marinating or as a barbecue sauce for outdoor grilling.

HOLLANDAISE SAUCE

The most beautiful sauce of all, this golden child of cooking is truly fit for a king, and many's the king who would have been hard put to choose between it and his favorite mistress. No need to think of such sacrifices nowadays, however, since Hollandaise sauce can be made with the twirl of a blender. Pity the king who doesn't have one. Marvelous for dressing up broccoli, asparagus, artichoke bottoms, hard cooked eggs, breast of chicken or fish.

INGREDIENTS

3 egg yolks
2 teaspoons lemon juice
½ cup sweet butter
pinch of salt and white pepper
1 cup hot water

ASSEMBLE

1 blender
1 cup
1 set measuring spoons
1 measuring cup
1 small saucepan

DIRECTIONS

Pour hot water into blender. Let stand one minute. Meanwhile separate 3 egg yolks and put in a cup. Empty blender. Put egg yolks, 2 teaspoons lemon juice, and a pinch each of salt and pepper into blender. Cover. Turn blender on high speed for a few seconds. Turn off. Melt ½ cup butter in saucepan. While butter is very hot, partially cover blender, turn on high and add butter in a steady stream. Do not pour in butter too rapidly. As soon as butter is completely added turn off blender motor. Serve immediately.

HERB-MINT SAUCE

A subtle sauce that's neither too plain nor too fancy. Try this spooned over cooked fish or broccoli for a dish that will delight you.

INGREDIENTS

1 egg yolk
1 tablespoon light cream
2 tablespoons dry sauterne
2 tablespoons butter
1 teaspoon tarragon (dried)
2 pinches each of crushed sweet
    basil, rosemary, nutmeg,
    thyme, salt, and pepper
¼ teaspoon mint flakes
1 cup hot water

ASSEMBLE

1 double boiler
1 cork screw
1 set measuring spoons
1 wire whisk or tablespoon
1 table knife

DIRECTIONS

Pour one cup hot water into bottom of double boiler. Place over medium high flame. Place the top of the double boiler over the bottom half. Then add butter, egg yolk, sauterne, and light cream. Beat with the wire whisk until the sauce begins to thicken. Add tarragon, salt, pepper, sweet basil, rosemary, thyme, and mint. Continue to whisk for two minutes.

COCONUT CREAM SAUCE

Creamy 3 ways is this Coconut Cream Sauce made from sweet cream, sour cream, and cream cheese. Serve over any cold, sweetened fruit. Fresh blackberries or canned figs are best.

INGREDIENTS

2 ounces cream cheese
¼ cup sour cream
4 tablespoons heavy sweet cream
5 tablespoons grated coconut

ASSEMBLE

1 mixing bowl
1 measuring cup
1 set measuring spoons
1 fork
1 tablespoon

DIRECTIONS

Place cream cheese and 4 tablespoons sweet cream in mixing bowl. Mash with fork, then stir rapidly until cream cheese is soft and creamy. Add ¼ cup sour cream. Mix, then beat until smooth. Add 5 tablespoons grated coconut. Stir. Serve cold.

MORNAY SAUCE

One of the hardest-working of all the classic French sauces. Tuck almost anything under a mantle of Mornay, sprinkle it with grated Swiss cheese, put it under a broiler for a minute, and voila! A creation worthy of the finest cook.

INGREDIENTS

3 tablespoons butter
3 tablespoons flour
1 cup milk
4 tablespoons heavy cream
½ cup grated Cheddar or Swiss
  cheese, packaged
¼ teaspoon parsley flakes
1 egg yolk
6 drops onion juice
2 pinches ground nutmeg
2 tablespoons canned instant
  whipped cream
salt and pepper to taste

ASSEMBLE

1 skillet
1 set measuring spoons
1 small saucepan
1 measuring cup
1 small mixing bowl
1 egg beater
1 tablespoon

DIRECTIONS

Heat one cup milk over high flame until scalding hot. Melt 3 tablespoons butter in skillet. Stir in the 3 tablespoons flour, 6 drops onion juice, ¼ teaspoon parsley flakes, ½ cup Cheddar or Swiss cheese, 2 pinches of nutmeg, and scalded milk. Stir until the cheese is melted and the sauce is smooth. In a bowl beat together the egg yolk and the heavy cream. Stir into sauce. Add salt and pepper to taste. Cook until sauce is smooth and thick. Be careful not to boil. Fold in the whipped cream. Especially good with shrimp, chicken, crab meat, oysters, eggs, broccoli, spinach, etc., etc., etc.

APRICOT SAUCE

This sauce is marvelous when heated and served over roast pork, chicken, game, or ham. For a complete about-face serve hot over vanilla or peach ice cream. Versatile, isn't it?

INGREDIENTS

1 7¾-ounce jar strained apricots for babies
2 tablespoons Grand Marnier or Cointreau
4 tablespoons butter
1 teaspoon honey

ASSEMBLE

1 jar opener
1 set measuring spoons
1 small saucepan or skillet
1 spoon

DIRECTIONS

Place all ingredients in saucepan. Bring to a boil over medium flame. Boil gently for 3 minutes, stirring constantly.

NOTE:

3 tablespoons undiluted consommé may be added if less sweetness is desired for use with meat.

RASPBERRY SAUCE

Berry meets berry in a tempting new way when Raspberry Sauce is poured over fresh, ripe strawberries. Or for a traditional treat, make Peach Melba in a minute by pouring this sauce over vanilla ice cream set on half a canned peach.

INGREDIENTS

½ 10-ounce package frozen raspberries, defrosted
1 tablespoon raspberry jelly

ASSEMBLE

1 blender
1 set measuring spoons
1 fine sieve
1 bowl

DIRECTIONS

Place berries in container of blender. Turn on high speed for one minute. Strain into bowl. Add 1 tablespoon raspberry jelly. Stir until smooth. Serve cold.

CHOCOLATE SAUCE

You'll be known for your chocolate sauce one minute after you serve this one. Really good chocolate sauces are as rare as the proverbial hen's proverbial teeth. Now you are the possessor of one of the most luscious. Bon appetit!

INGREDIENTS

2 squares bitter chocolate
1 tablespoon butter
½ cup sugar
½ cup light cream
½ teaspoon vanilla

ASSEMBLE

1 small heavy skillet
1 tablespoon
1 set measuring spoons
1 mixing bowl
1 measuring cup

DIRECTIONS

Place chocolate squares and butter in small heavy skillet. Melt chocolate over low flame. In mixing bowl combine sugar and cream. Add to melted chocolate. Stir over medium low flame until sauce reaches boiling point. Reduce heat. Cook over low flame until sauce thickens slightly. Stir in vanilla. Serve hot or cold.

Menus

The perfect this to go with that

In a book where many things have been made much of it may seem contradictory to say that menu-making is *the* most important aspect of serving a really superb meal. If you think back on what has preceded, however, you will remember that one of the first statements made in this book was ". . . cooking is easy. If you can read you can cook." This being true, it will not seem amiss to emphasize the prominent role menus play in the art of feeding yourself and your guests not only properly but expertly.

The capacity for choosing the perfect this to go with the perfect that when constructing a meal was discussed in the forewords on soups, salads, vegetables, entrées, etc., but to bring the whole subject into sharper focus, it may help to remember the following:

1. *The entrée*

Should be selected first.

Should take into consideration the preferences or prejudices of your guests if known to you.

Should be consistent with the time of the year. Serve lighter foods in summer or smaller portions of richer foods.

Should be appropriate for the occasion. The more important the occasion, the more elaborate the meal and the more carefully constructed the menu.

2. *Hors d'oeuvres*

Should complement the entrée both in texture and in flavor.

Should not overpower the main course in quantity, flavor, or flamboyance, or you may find the rest of your meal anticlimactic.

Should be impressive enough in taste and appearance to draw the attention of your guest or guests away from animated political or business discussions. Dinner is much more enjoyable if conversation is lively but not too controversial and disturbing.

3. *The soup*

Should contain elements complementary to both the hors d'oeuvre and the entrée.

Should provide a change of pace. If hors d'oeuvre and entrée are attention-getters, the soup should be soothing and restful to prepare the way for the main course. On the other hand, if the hors d'oeuvre and entrée are rich but bland, the soup should have sufficient personality to open eyes and alert palates for the coming treat. But again, caution! The main course is still the star!

4. *The salad*

Should offer a change of flavor and texture to heighten the pleasure of the main course. As the soup prepares the palate for the main course, so the salad cools, refreshes, and offers a change of pace during the meal itself. It should, therefore, complement the flavors of the entrée and offer a stimulating taste change without completely submerging the subtleties of the main course.

5. The vegetable

Should be tasteful padding to round out the meal as well as to provide an interesting taste treat.

Should be completely subservient to the entrée. Not too similar to, not too different from the main course. If your choice of vegetables is perfect they will be greatly enjoyed but seldom remembered. Your guest should be so blinded by the beauty of the main course that while relishing every bite of vegetable, he is hard put to remember exactly what it was that seemed so delightful.

6. The Dessert

Should be the only element in the meal that can rival the entrée.

Should still rely upon the main course for inspiration. Although the dessert can be a marvelous attention getter, it must be chosen to complement the meal it follows. A delicate meal relying upon subtlety for its impact can afford to close with a creamy, sensuous dessert. However, a meal rich in its textures and flavors seems to cry out for a light, fruity dessert such as Pêches Flambées. Desserts can be dramatic and different but must be perfectly suited to the meals they conclude.

BRUNCHES

The following combinations are ideal for brunch!

I.

Curried Pineapple Slices
Creamy Scrambled Eggs with Truffles
Toast Points

II.

Glazed Apple Slices
Greek Pontica

III.

Chilled Tomato Juice with Pepper
Clam Hash

IV

Chilled Clam Juice
Eggs with Cherry Tomatoes
Rye Toast Points

V.

Strawberry Juice
Apple Pancake

VI.

Fried Bananas
Fluffy Corn Fritters
(with Maple Syrup)

LUNCHES

(Lunch is generally served with an hors d'oeuvre *or* soup)

CHICKEN PRINCESSE

May be served with a choice of the following:

HORS D'OEUVRE:
 Eggs à la Russe
 Fresh Mushrooms in Double Cream

SOUPS:
 Garlic Soup with Croutons and Poached Egg
 Tomato Crab Bisque
 Curried Lemon Soup
 Jellied Madrilene in Avocado Shells
 Chilly Crème de Menthe Soup

SALADS:
 Cucumber Salad Damascus
 Cauliflower Salad

VEGETABLES:
 Carrots and White Grapes
 New Peas with Mint
 Cauliflower with Almonds
 Potato Pflutters
 Artichokes with Foie Gras

GO WITHS:

Grilled Cheese Tomatoes
Petite Peas in Artichoke Bottoms
Curried Pineapple Slices

DESSERTS:

Pêches Flambées
Apple Cointreau Sundae
Strawberry Trifle
Sherbet in Orange Cups

LOBSTER SALAD

May be served with a choice of the following:

HORS D'OEUVRE:

    Fresh Figs and Walnuts in Prosciutto Ham
    Fresh Vegetables with Tuna Dip

SOUPS:

    Jellied Madrilene in Avocado Shells
    Tomato Crab Bisque
    Curried Lemon Soup
    Chilly Crème de Menthe Soup

GO WITHS:

    Ham Cornucopias
    Anchovies in Cherry Tomatoes

DESSERTS:

    Pêches Flambées
    Apple Pancake
    Apple Cointreau Sundae
    Cherries Jubilee Sundae
    Strawberry Trifle
    Greek Pontica
    Sherbet in Orange Cups
    Mousse au Chocolat

ASPARAGUS AND EGG WITH CHEDDAR CHEESE
May be served with a choice of the following:

HORS D'OEUVRE:
Vegetables à la Grecque
French Vegetables with Tuna Dip

SOUPS:
Jellied Madrilene in Avocado Shells
Tomato Crab Bisque

SALADS:
Cauliflower Salad
Bibb Lettuce with Antipasto Dressing

VEGETABLES:
Garlic Cherry Tomatoes
Green Beans Serbian
Vegetables in Cream
Green Beans au Beurre
Potato Pflutters
Baked Stuffed Cheese Potatoes

GO WITHS:
Grilled Cheese Tomatoes
Anchovies in Cherry Tomatoes

DESSERTS:
Apple Cointreau Sundae
Greek Pontica
Sherbet in Orange Cups

SAUTÉED PÂTÉ DE FOIE GRAS AND SWISS CHEESE SANDWICH

May be served with a choice of the following:

HORS D'OEUVRES:

Fresh Mushrooms in Double Cream
Fresh Figs and Walnuts in Prosciutto Ham
Fresh Vegetables with Tuna Dip

SOUPS:

Garlic Soup with Croutons and Poached Egg
Jellied Madrilene in Avocado Shells
Tomato Crab Bisque
Curried Lemon Soup
Gazpacho

SALADS:

Cucumber Salad Damascus
Fruit and Cucumber Salad
Cauliflower Salad
Caesar Salad
Cold String Bean and Shrimp Salad
Coquille St. Jacques Salad

GO WITHS:

Anchovies in Cherry Tomatoes
Grilled Cheese Tomatoes
Petite Peas in Artichoke Bottoms
Curried Pineapple Slices

DESSERTS:

Pêches Flambées
Apple Cointreau Sundae
Sherbet in Orange Cups
Mousse au Chocolat

MOZZARELLA IN CARROZZA
May be served with a choice of the following:

HORS D'OEUVRE:

Italian Antipasto
Fresh Figs and Walnuts in Prosciutto Ham
Fresh Vegetables with Tuna Dip

SOUPS:

Garlic Soup with Croutons and Poached Egg
Tomato Crab Bisque
Gazpacho

SALADS:

Italian White Bean and Anchovy Salad
Caesar Salad
Onion Salad
Cucumber Salad Damascus
Cauliflower Salad
Asparagus and Smoked Salmon Salad

GO WITHS:

Anchovies in Cherry Tomatoes

DESSERTS:

Sherbet in Orange Cups

EGGS FLORENTINE

May be served with a choice of the following:

HORS D'OEUVRE:

Fresh Mushrooms in Double Cream
Fresh Vegetables with Tuna Dip

SOUPS:

Jellied Madrilene in Avocado Shells
Tomato Crab Bisque
Curried Lemon Soup
Chilly Creme de Menthe Soup

SALADS:

Cucumber Salad Damascus
Cauliflower Salad
Cold String Beans and Shrimp Salad

VEGETABLES:

Garlic Cherry Tomatoes
Green Onions with Lemon Clam Sauce
Carrots and White Grapes
Cauliflower with Almonds

GO WITHS:

Anchovies in Cherry Tomatoes
Grilled Cheese Tomatoes
Petite Peas in Artichoke Bottoms

DESSERTS:

Pêches Flambées
Sherbet in Orange Cups
Mousse au Chocolat

ENTRÉES

BREAST OF CHICKEN IN RUM CRUMBS
May be served with a choice of the following:

HORS D'OEUVRE:
   Mushrooms Stuffed with Walnuts and Pistachios, Glazed
   Fresh Figs and Walnuts in Prosciutto Ham

SOUPS:
   Cream of Asparagus with Asparagus Tips and Anchovy
      Croutons
   Curried Lemon Soup
   Cold Old German Fruit Soup in Cantaloupe Shells
   Jellied Madrilene in Avocado Shells
   Chilly Crème de Menthe Soup

SALADS:
   Fruit and Cucumber Salad
   Cauliflower Salad

VEGETABLES:
   Fluffy Corn Fritters
   Green Beans Serbian
   Carrots and White Grapes
   Vegetables in Cream
   Green Beans and Onions Au Beurre

GO WITHS:
   Petite Peas in Artichoke Bottoms
   Curried Pineapple

Fried Bananas
Marrons and Apricots
Glazed Apple Rings

DESSERTS:

Pêches Flambées
Apple Pancake
Crêpes Suzette
Apple Cointreau Sundae
Cherry Jubilee Sundae
Cold Old German Fruit Soup in Cantaloupe Shells

LOBSTER PERNOD OR
ABSINTHE GOURMET
May be served with a choice of the following:

HORS D'OEUVRE:

Vegetables à la Grecque

Hors d'oeuvre tray, consisting of Fresh Mushrooms in Double Cream, Eggs à la Russe, Italian White Bean and Anchovy Salad, and Vegetables à la Grecque

Mushrooms Stuffed with Walnuts and Pistachios, Glazed

Ramekins of Shrimp in Sour Cream

SOUPS:

Jellied Madrilene in Avocado Shells

Tomato Crab Bisque

Cream of Asparagus Soup with Asparagus Tips and Anchovy Croutons

SALADS:

Cucumber Salad Damascus

Cold String Bean and Shrimp Salad

Bibb Lettuce with Green Goddess Dressing

VEGETABLES:

New Peas with Mint

Green Beans and Onions Au Beurre

Grilled Cheese Tomatoes

Petite Peas in Artichoke Bottoms

DESSERTS:

Pêches Flambées

Apple Cointreau Sundae

Sherbet in Orange Cups

BOEUF AU VIN BLANC
May be served with a choice of the following:

HORS D'OEUVRE:

Vegetables à la Grecque
Fresh Mushrooms in Double Cream
Escargots in Cream
Mushrooms Stuffed with Walnuts and Pistachios, Glazed

SOUPS:

Garlic Soup with Croutons and Poached Egg
Real French Onion Soup
Cream of Asparagus Soup with Asparagus Tips and Anchovy Croutons

SALADS:

Cucumber Salad Damascus
Onion Salad
Bibb Lettuce with Green Goddess Dressing
Caesar Salad

VEGETABLES:

Garlic Cherry Tomatoes
Green Beans Serbian
Carrots and White Grapes
New Peas with Mint
Green Beans and Onions au Beurre
Fried Green Peppers
Potato Pflutters
Baked Stuffed Cheese Potatoes

GO WITHS:

Anchovies in Cherry Tomatoes
Grilled Cheese Tomatoes

DESSERTS:

    Pêches Flambées
    Apple Cointreau Sundae
    Sherbet in Orange Cups
    Mousse au Chocolat

CALF'S LIVER PARIS
May be served with a choice of the following:

HORS D'OEUVRE:

Vegetables à la Grecque
Mushrooms Stuffed with Walnuts and Pistachios, Glazed
Fresh Figs and Walnuts in Prosciutto Ham

SOUPS:

Garlic Soup with Croutons and Poached Egg
Jellied Madrilene in Avocado Shells
Tomato Crab Bisque
Cream of Asparagus Soup with Asparagus Tips and Anchovy Croutons
Chilly Crème de Menthe Soup

SALADS:

Cucumber Salad Damascus
Fruit and Cucumber Salad
Cauliflower Salad

VEGETABLES:

Carrots and White Grapes
Vegetables in Cream
Green Beans and Onions au Beurre
Fried Green Peppers
Artichokes with Foie Gras

GO WITHS:

Anchovies in Cherry Tomatoes
Petite Peas in Artichoke Bottoms
Glazed Apple Rings

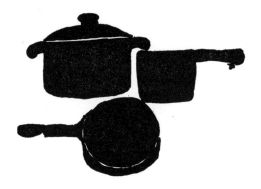

DESSERTS:
    Pêches Flambées
    Cherries Jubilee Sundae
    Apple Cointreau Sundae

LOBSTER-SHRIMP OR CRAYFISH
IN WINE RICE

May be served with a choice of the following:

HORS D'OEUVRE:

Vegetables à la Grecque
Fresh Vegetables with Tuna Dip
Fresh Mushrooms in Double Cream
Coquille St. Jacques

SOUPS:

Jellied Madrilene in Avocado Shells
Tomato Crab Bisque
Cream of Asparagus Soup with Asparagus Tips and Anchovy Croutons

SALADS:

Cucumber Salad Damascus
Cauliflower Salad
Bibb Lettuce with Green Goddess Dressing

VEGETABLES:

New Peas with Mint
Vegetables in Cream
Green Beans and Onions au Beurre
Fried Green Peppers

GO WITHS:

Petite Peas in Artichoke Bottoms

DESSERTS:

Pêches Flambées
Sherbet in Orange Cups
Champagne Fruit Cocktail

BOUILLABAISSE

May be served with a choice of the following:

HORS D'OEUVRE:

Vegetables à la Grecque

Hors d'oeuvre tray, consisting of Eggs à la Russe, Vegetables à la Grecque, Fresh Mushrooms in Double Cream, and Italian White Bean and Anchovy Salad

Mushrooms Stuffed with Walnuts and Pistachios, Glazed

Escargots in Cream

SOUPS:

No soup is needed as Bouillabaisse is a soup as well as a seafood dinner

SALADS:

Cucumber Salad Damascus

Italian White Bean and Anchovy Salad

Onion Salad

Caesar Salad

VEGETABLES:

Green Beans Serbian

Green Onions with Lemon Clam Sauce

New Peas with Mint

Green Beans and Onions au Beurre

DESSERTS:

Apple Cointreau Sundae

Pêches Flambées

Sherbet in Orange Cups

Mousse au Chocolat

SHRIMP CURRY

May be served with a choice of the following:

HORS D'OEUVRE:

Mushrooms Stuffed with Walnuts and Pistachios, Glazed
Fresh Figs and Walnuts in Prosciutto Ham

SOUPS:

Garlic Soup with Croutons and Poached Egg
Jellied Madrilene in Avocado Shells
Tomato Crab Bisque
Chilly Crème de Menthe Soup

SALADS:

Cucumber Salad Damascus
Onion Salad
Lebanese Salad
Fruit and Cucumber Salad
Cauliflower Salad

VEGETABLES:

Garlic Cherry Tomatoes
Green Beans Serbian
Green Onions with Lemon Clam Sauce
Carrots and White Grapes
New Peas with Mint
Cauliflower with Almonds
Vegetables in Cream
Green Beans and Onions au Beurre
Fried Green Peppers

GO WITHS:

Curried Pineapple
Fried Bananas

Flaming Spiced Peaches
Marrons and Apricots

DESSERTS:

Pêches Flambées
Strawberry Trifle
Sherbet in Orange Cups
Apple Cointreau Sundae

KIDNEYS FLAMBÉ

May be served with a choice of the following:

HORS D'OEUVRE:

Mushrooms Stuffed with Walnuts and Pistachios, Glazed
Fresh Figs and Walnuts in Prosciutto Ham

SOUPS:

Garlic Soup with Croutons and Poached Egg
Jellied Madrilene in Avocado Shells
Real French Onion Soup
Chilly Crème de Menthe Soup

SALADS:

Cucumber Salad Damascus
Cauliflower Salad
Onion Salad
Bibb Lettuce with Green Goddess or Capered French
    Dressing
Caesar Salad

VEGETABLES:

Vegetables in Cream
Green Beans and Onions au Beurre
Fried Green Peppers
Garlic Cherry Tomatoes
Green Beans Serbian
Carrots and White Grapes
New Peas with Mint
Cauliflower with Almonds
Potato Pflutters
Baked Stuffed Cheese Potatoes

GO WITHS:

    Glazed Apple Rings
    Grilled Cheese Tomatoes
    Petite Peas in Artichoke Bottoms

DESSERTS:

    Apple Pancake
    Apple Cointreau Sundae
    Cherry Jubilee Sundae
    Mousse au Chocolat
    Sherbet in Orange Cups
    Cold Old German Fruit Soup in Cantaloupe Shells

SPAGHETTI WITH WHITE CLAM SAUCE
May be served with a choice of the following:

HORS D'OEUVRE:

Italian Antipasto
Vegetables à la Grecque
Fresh Figs and Walnuts in Prosciutto Ham
Mozzarella in Carrozza

SOUPS:

Garlic Soup with Croutons and Poached Egg

SALADS:

Italian White Bean and Anchovy Salad
Onion Salad
Cauliflower Salad
Cold String Bean and Shrimp Salad

VEGETABLES:

Garlic Cherry Tomatoes
Green Beans Serbian
Green Beans and Onions au Beurre
Fried Green Peppers

GO WITHS:

Anchovies in Cherry Tomatoes, except when using Anchovy Salad

DESSERTS:

Sherbet in Orange Cups

BREAST OF CHICKEN PERIGOURDINE
May be served with a choice of the following:

HORS D'OEUVRE:

    Vegetables à la Grecque
    Fresh Mushrooms in Double Cream
    Mushrooms Stuffed with Walnuts and Pistachios, Glazed
    Fresh Figs and Walnuts in Prosciutto Ham
    Coquille St. Jacques

SOUPS:

    Jellied Madrilene in Avocado Shells
    Tomato Crab Bisque
    Real French Onion Soup
    Cream of Asparagus with Asparagus Tips and Anchovy
        Croutons

SALADS:

    Cucumber Salad Damascus
    Fruit and Cucumber Salad
    Cold String Beans and Shrimp Salad

VEGETABLES:

    Green Beans Serbian
    Green Onions with Lemon Clam Sauce
    Carrots and White Grapes
    New Peas and Onions au Beurre
    Potato Pflutters

DESSERTS:

    Crêpes Suzette
    Pêches Flambées
    Mousse au Chocolat
    Sherbet in Orange Cups

ESCARGOTS BOURGUIGNONNE
May be served with a choice of the following:

HORS D'OEUVRE:

Vegetables à la Grecque
Fresh Mushrooms in Double Cream
Mushrooms Stuffed with Walnuts and Pistachios, Glazed
Coquille St. Jacques

SOUPS:

Jellied Madrilene in Avocado Shells
Real French Onion Soup

SALADS:

Cucumber Salad Damascus
Cauliflower Salad
Bibb Lettuce with Green Goddess Dressing
Caesar Salad

VEGETABLES:

Green Beans Serbian
New Peas with Mint
Vegetables in Cream
Green Beans and Onions au Beurre

DESSERTS:

Crêpes Suzette
Pêches Flambées
Apple Cointreau Sundae
Sherbet in Orange Cups
Mousse au Chocolat

SHRIMPS FLAMBÉ
May be served with a choice of the following:

HORS D'OEUVRE:
Mushrooms Stuffed with Walnuts and Pistachios, Glazed
Fresh Figs and Walnuts in Prosciutto Ham
Coquille St. Jacques

SOUPS:
Jellied Madrilene in Avocado Shells
Real French Onion Soup
Cream of Asparagus Soup with Asparagus Tips and Anchovy Croutons

SALADS:
Cucumber Salad Damascus
Cauliflower Salad
Fruit and Cucumber Salad

VEGETABLES:
Green Beans Serbian
Green Onions with Lemon Clam Sauce
New Peas with Mint
Vegetables in Cream
Green Beans and Onions au Beurre
Artichokes with Foie Gras
Grilled Cheese Tomatoes
Petite Peas in Artichoke Bottoms

DESSERTS:
Pêches Flambées
Sherbet in Orange Cups
Mousse au Chocolat

SHRIMPS SCAMPI

May be served with a choice of the following:

HORS D'OEUVRE:

Italian Antipasto
Vegetables à la Grecque
Mozzarella in Carrozza

SOUPS:

Jellied Madrilene in Avocado Shells
Tomato Crab Bisque
Gazpacho
Curried Lemon Soup
Chilly Crème de Menthe Soup

SALADS:

Italian White Bean and Anchovy Salad
Cucumber Salad Damascus
Onion Salad
Cauliflower Salad
Lebanese Salad
Caesar Salad

VEGETABLES:

Green Beans Serbian
Green Onions with Lemon Clam Sauce
New Peas with Mint
Green Beans and Onions au Beurre
Fried Green Peppers
Grilled Cheese Tomatoes
Potato Pflutters

GO WITHS:

Anchovies in Cherry Tomatoes

DESSERTS:

Pêches Flambées
Greek Pontica
Sherbet in Orange Cups

DANISH FISH WITH BLUE CHEESE
May be served with a choice of the following:

HORS D'OEUVRE:

Vegetables à la Grecque
Eggs à la Russe

SOUPS:

Jellied Madrilene in Avocado Shells
Garlic Soup with Croutons and Poached Egg
Cream of Asparagus with Asparagus Tips and Anchovy
    Croutons
Curried Lemon Soup

SALADS:

Onion Salad
Cucumber Salad Damascus
Cold String Bean and Shrimp Salad

VEGETABLES:

Vegetables in Cream
Green Beans and Onions au Beurre
Fried Green Peppers
Green Beans Serbian
New Peas with Mint
Potato Pflutters

DESSERTS:

Pêches Flambées
Apple Cointreau Sundae

COOKING OUT GOURMET STYLE

CHICKEN LIVERS AND WHITE GRAPES
May be served with a choice of the following:

HORS D'OEUVRE:
Fresh Mushrooms in Double Cream
Mushrooms Stuffed with Walnuts and Pistachios, Glazed
Fresh Figs and Walnuts in Prosciutto Ham

SALADS:
Cucumber Salad Damascus
Fruit and Cucumber Salad

VEGETABLES:
Green Beans Serbian
New Peas with Mint
Cauliflower with Almonds

GO WITHS:
Glazed Apple Rings
Flaming Spiced Peaches
Marrons and Apricots
Petite Peas in Artichoke Bottoms
Curried Pineapple Slices

DESSERTS:
Champagne Fruit Cocktail
Pêches Flambées
Apple Pancake

Apple Cointreau Sundae
Cherries Jubilee Sundae
Fruit en Brochette
Sherbet in Orange Cups
Cold Old German Fruit Soup

SCALLOPS AND CHERRY TOMATOES
May be served with a choice of the following:

HORS D'OEUVRE:

Italian Antipasto
Vegetables à la Grecque
Fresh Vegetables in Tuna Dip
Pineapple, Shrimp, Chicken Livers, and Olives en Brochette

SALADS:

Italian White Bean and Anchovy Salad
Onion Salad
Cauliflower Salad
Lebanese Salad
Caesar Salad
Asparagus and Smoked Salmon Salad
Coquille St. Jacques Salad

VEGETABLES:

Green Beans Serbian
Baked Cheese Potatoes
Green Onions with Lemon Clam Sauce
New Peas with Mint
Fried Green Peppers

DESSERTS:

Fruit en Brochette
Sherbet in Orange Cups
Cherries Jubilee Sundae

STEAK KEBOBS
May be served with a choice of the following:

HORS D'OEUVRE:
Italian Antipasto
Vegetables à la Grecque
Pineapple, Shrimp, Chicken Livers, and Olives en Brochette

SALADS:
Cucumber Salad Damascus
Onion Salad
Lebanese Salad
Cauliflower Salad
Italian White Bean and Anchovy Salad
Caesar Salad

VEGETABLES:
Garlic Cherry Tomatoes
Green Beans Serbian
Baked Stuffed Cheese Potatoes

DESSERTS:
Fruit en Brochette
Apple Cointreau Sundae
Cherries Jubilee Sundae
Sherbet in Orange Cups

GINGER-SHRIMP KEBOBS
May be served with a choice of the following:

HORS D'OEUVRE:
Italian Antipasto
Eggs à la Russe
Fresh Vegetables with Tuna Dip

SALADS:
Cucumber Salad Damascus
Lebanese Salad
Cauliflower Salad
Caesar Salad

VEGETABLES:
Garlic Cherry Tomatoes
Green Beans Serbian
Green Beans and Onions au Beurre
Fried Green Peppers

DESSERTS:
Pêches Flambées
Fruit en Brochette
Sherbet in Orange Cups

CHICKEN, PINEAPPLE, AND
SWEET POTATO KEBOBS
May be served with a choice of the following:

HORS D'OEUVRE:

Eggs à la Russe
Fresh Figs and Walnuts in Prosciutto Ham
Mushrooms Stuffed with Walnuts and Pistachios, Glazed

SALADS:

Cucumber Salad Damascus
Fruit and Cucumber Salad
Cauliflower Salad

VEGETABLES:

Fluffy Corn Fritters
Green Beans Serbian
Carrots and White Grapes

GO WITHS:

Flaming Spiced Peaches
Fried Bananas

DESSERTS:

Apple Cointreau Sundae
Cherries Jubilee Sundae
Fruit en Brochette
Sherbet in Orange Cups

MIDNIGHT SNACKS

CREAMED CRAB MEAT AND OYSTERS
May be served with a choice of the following:

SALADS:
Cucumber Salad Damascus
Fruit and Cucumber Salad
Cauliflower Salad
Caesar Salad
Cold String Bean and Shrimp Salad

VEGETABLES:
Garlic Cherry Tomatoes
Green Onions with Lemon Clam Sauce
Carrots and White Grapes
New Peas with Mint
Vegetables in Cream
Green Beans and Onions au Beurre
Artichokes with Foie Gras

GO WITHS:
Anchovies in Cherry Tomatoes
Petite Peas in Artichoke Bottoms

DESSERTS:
Crêpes Suzette
Pêches Flambées
Apple Cointreau Sundae
Sherbet in Orange Cups
Mousse au Chocolat

LOBSTER À LA NEWBURG
May be served with a choice of the following:

SALADS:
Cucumber Salad Damascus
Cauliflower Salad
Caesar Salad
Cold String Bean and Shrimp Salad

VEGETABLES:
Green Onions with Lemon Clam Sauce
Carrots and White Grapes
New Peas with Mint
Vegetables in Cream
Green Beans and Onions au Beurre
Artichokes with Foie Gras

GO WITHS:
Grilled Cheese Tomatoes
Petite Peas in Artichoke Bottoms

DESSERTS:
Sherbet in Orange Cups
Champagne Fruit Cocktail
Crêpes Suzette
Pêches Flambées
Apple Cointreau Sundae
Cherries Jubilee Sundae

SWISS FONDUE
   May be served with a choice of the following:

DESSERTS:
   Champagne Fruit Cocktail
   Pêches Flambées

LOBSTER STEW
   May be served with a choice of the following:

SALADS:
   Caesar Salad
   Cold String Bean and Shrimp Salad

DESSERT:
   Sherbet in Orange Cups

SUKIYAKI

May be served with a choice of the following:

SALADS:

Cucumber Salad Damascus
Cold String Bean and Shrimp Salad

DESSERTS:

Sherbet in Orange Cups
Fruit en Brochette
Apple Cointreau Sundae

WELSH RAREBIT
May be served with a choice of the following:

SALADS:

Cucumber Salad Damascus
Caesar Salad
Cold String Bean and Shrimp Salad

VEGETABLES:

Green Beans Serbian
New Peas with Mint

GO WITHS:

Grilled Cheese Tomatoes
Petite Peas in Artichoke Bottoms

DESSERTS:

Pêches Flambées
Sherbet in Orange Cups
Mousse au Chocolat

BE VERSATILE

Frequently dishes can be used interchangeably. For example, Ramekins of Shrimp in Sour Cream, which is often served as an hors d'oeuvre, nimbly turns into a Midnight Snack when served at the witching hour. Following are others that are equally versatile.

May be served as a main course for

MIDNIGHT SNACKS	LUNCHES
Shrimp Curry	Fruit and Cucumber Salad
Spaghetti with White Clam Sauce	Shrimp Curry
Caesar Salad	Caesar Salad
Champagne Fruit Cocktail	Tartar Sandwiches
Tartar Sandwiches	Escargots in Cream
Escargots in Cream	Potato Clam Chowder
Eggs Florentine	Ramekins of Shrimp in Sour Cream
Ramekins of Shrimp in Sour Cream	Lobster Stew
Shrimps Flambé	Danish Fish with Blue Cheese
Shrimps Scampi	Shrimps Flambé
Escargots Bourguignonne	Shrimps Scampi
Boeuf au Vin Blanc	Coquille St. Jacques

Index